MAKBARA

Also by Juan Goytisolo

MAKBARA

JUAN GOYTISOLO

Translated from the Spanish by
HELEN R. LANE

SEAVER BOOKS ================ NEW YORK

First Edition 1981
First Printing 1981
ISBN: 0-394-51803-9   Seaver Books ISBN: 0-86579-014-0
Library of Congress Catalog Card Number: 81-5808

LIBRARY OF CONGRESS CATALOGING IN PUBLICATION DATA
Goytisolo, Juan.
Makbara.
I. Title.
PQ6613.O79M313   863'.64   81-5808
ISBN 0-394-51803-9   AACR2

Designed by Beth Tondreau
Manufactured in the United States of America
Distributed by Grove Press, Inc., New York
SEAVER BOOKS, 333 Central Park West, New York, N.Y. 10025

To those who inspired it
and will not read it

In the icy waters of egoistic calculation
Karl Marx, *Communist Manifesto*

all this the world well knowes
yet none knowes well,
to shun the heaven that leads men
to this hell.
William Shakespeare, Sonnet 129

منثل الريح بـﻓ الشبكة
Moroccan Proverb

CONTENTS

xi

MAKBARA

COME FROM THE NETHER WORLD

in the beginning was the cry: alarm, anguish, terror, chemically pure pain?: prolonged, sustained, piercing, to the limits of the tolerable: phantom, specter, monster from the nether world: a disturbing intrusion at any event: disruption of the urban rhythm, of the harmonious chorus of sounds and voices of supernumeraries and beautifully dressed actors and actresses: an oneiric apparition: an insolent, brutish defiance: a strange, transgressive presence: a radical negation of the existing order: index finger pointed accusingly at the happy, self-confident Eurocraticonsuming city: with no need to raise his eyes, strain his voice, extend his beggar's hand with a black gesture of Luciferian pride: absorbed in the obverse side of the spectacle he is creating: indifferent to the horror he inspires as he passes by: a virus contaminating the collective body of the city in the wake of his delirious journey through it: dusky, bare feet, insensitive to the rigors of the season: ragged, threadbare pants with improvised skylights at the knees: a scarecrow's overcoat with the collar raised to conceal a double absence: walking, lost in self-contemplation, down the sidewalk of the boulevard teeming with humanity: past the tobacco store, the haberdasher's shop, the rue du Sentier intersection, the terrace of the café-restaurant, the slot-machine parlor: the usual line outside the Ciné Rex, the entrance to the Bonne-Nouvelle métro station, the newspaper stand, the street stall of the candy and ice cream vendor: past the eternally flag-bedecked building of the very official spokesman of the working class: unhurriedly making his way through the crowd with no need to elbow anyone aside: by virtue of the sheer and simple power of his corrosive presence: did you see that, mama?: for heaven's sake, don't stare like that!: I can't believe it!: can't you see you're embarrassing that man, darling?: don't stand there gaping like an idiot, I tell you: what's he got on his face?: shut up, not another word out of you!: it's incredible how they let them run around loose!: he's stumbling along like he was dead drunk!: he looks like some kind of a nut!: don't talk so loud, he might hear you!: watch out, don't brush up against him!: all of them ought to be sent back to where they came from!: that's for sure, but it'd be us taxpayers who paid for their tickets!: the Nazis had the right idea!: I'm sure he's got syphilis!: suddenly confronted with the Christmas bear that is an advertising gimmick for the enormously popular Walt Disney films being shown: the object of the affectionate attention of the flock of kids that all the ballyhoo has drawn to the place: going down the zigzagging line of papas and mamas with their smiling offspring in their arms: an enlarged replica of those jolly plush teddy bears that sit on children's beds in cozy bourgeois dwellings: a flat-footed, carnivorous mammal, with a massive, clumsy body, a thick pelt, huge strong paws, stout curving claws: a solitary inhabitant of cold countries, intelligent, astute, clever, with proverbial boldness and courage in dangerous moments and situations: reduced to a puppet thanks to his makeup man, complete with touches of appealing Hollywood-style innocence: a total absence of any sign of balls in the hircine groin: completely shorn of the most noble attributes of his lusty temperament: the two creatures

3

face to face now, with just a trace of mutual astonishment: time enough to exchange a polite, neutral look: another thoroughly tamed body, totally subservient to them: shame, humiliation, disgust, and they call this living!: paying, forever paying, a roof over your head, heat, sleep, food, paying, paying, is that what we came into this world for?: abandoning him finally to his awkward movements: to the venal exercise of his ridiculous cheeriness: dodging the motionless bumpers of the cars on the rue Poissonnière and over onto the opposite sidewalk: the de luxe terrace of the Madeleine Bastille: escorted by the pitiless gaze of candidates for Walt Disney's beatific technicolor: dusky feet on the ice-cold cement: walking on and on, as always: in a world apart from the mute rejection of those passing by in the opposite direction: from the simpleminded prudence that causes them to move aside so as to avoid all contact: from the aseptic, circumspect fear on their deliberately blank faces: go on, that's it, go on, don't stop, don't pay any attention, act as though you're blind, never meet their gaze, the walking leper, the monster, the carrier of the plague is you, is you, is you: crossing the intersection of Notre Dame de Recouvrance, the stupendous bargains of a remnant store blaring out canned music: the rue de la Ville Neuve, with the arrow pointing to the movie theater and the poster advertising

4

the tempting program: DOUBLES PÉNÉTRA-
TIONS, JEUNES FILLES EN CHALEUR: LE
RYTHME MAXI-PORNO DES SCÈNES VOUS
FERA JOUIR!: yet another café terrace: half a dozen
tables protected from the cold by thick plate glass: an
illuminated aquarium, with a self-satisfied white-
waterlily clientele: a theater box that becomes part of
the stage décor and offers a privileged spot from
which to view the enigmatic apparition: the passage
of the immigrant of astonishing countenance: dusky,
bare feet, insensitive to the rigors of the season: ragged, threadbare pants with improvised skylights at
the knees: a scarecrow's overcoat with the collar
raised to conceal a double absence: myself: an image
come from the nether world: apparently incapable of
objectivizing his situation except in monetary terms,
daiman el flus, an eternal cash-flow problem: immune
to the malicious comments of the crowd on the sidewalk: un fou probablement, qu'est-ce qui peut se pas-
ser dans sa tête?: bursting out laughing to himself: as
if they didn't know!: as if they didn't know the
thoughts running through my head!: shame, humiliation, disgust, and they call this living!: or are they
blind too perhaps?: going past the corner of the rue
Thorel, two city policewomen in eggplant-colored
uniforms: absorbed in the task of filling out tickets
for the cars illegally parked along the street: also sur-

prised and uneasy when they finally stop and take a
good look at you: tu ne crois pas qu'il faudrait prévenir le Commissaire?: laisse tomber, on a presque
fini, je veux rentrer à l'heure: but their eyes following
him nonetheless as he walks on, past the watch shop
and the optometrist's, I skirt a redyellowblack Kodak
rhombohedron, detour around the strategic advance
patrol of a tailor shop whose mannequins have over-
run the sidewalk: pass by the tobacco shop, the flower
stall, the employment agency: walking on and on and
on like a robot: shielding oneself in the horror that
one arouses as though it were a suit of armor: if only
my eyes could shoot flames: nothing behind me,
everything dead as I pass by: fire, everything on fire:
the display windows, the shops, the cars, the houses,
the people living in them: scrap iron, bones, ruins, a
cemetery, nothing but scorched earth: a bald gentleman in a fur coat, family groups, five abreast, that
break ranks when they meet up with you, dropping
each other's gloved hands: tu as vu sa tête, papa?: oui,
mon petit, c'est rien, ne le regarde pas comme ça, c'est
mal élevé: another heated terrace, the two-dimen-
sional silhouette of a chef with a white toque holding
up a list of the dishes on the special tourist menu: the
innocent astonishment on children's faces, furtive
grimaces, sidelong glances: the pariah, the plague carrier, the black: moving about freely, watching us

without looking at us, giving the appearance of hatching some secret plot, feeling proud of the terror he arouses in us: where does he come from?: who has let him out to run around loose, in rags and covered with sores, instead of putting him in quarantine under very strict medical surveillance?: a menace, a provocation, an attempt to mobilize against him the defensive reflexes of a society that is liberal and tolerant, but resolved to fight tooth and nail against anything that threatens law and order and the peace of mind of the family?: a bad egg, a black sheep, a dissonant parasite: an improperly tuned instrument in the execution of a score: a metaphor lost amid the algebraic signs of an equation: a computer that instead of providing the answer required by a committee of financial experts turns its data into a violent antimilitarist poem!: past the pharmacy, the entrance to the métro station, the photography studio, the haberdasher's shop: up the ramp whose stone parapet, there where the rue de la Lune and the rue Cléry meet, gradually channels the flow of pedestrian traffic along the boulevard: down the other side of it, clinging to the handrail, without so much as a glance at the ancient, venerable bulk of the Porte Saint-Denis: forcing those coming toward you from the opposite direction to move aside for you: they stare at you in amazement as they pass by you and then turn and look back at you with expressions of loathing and alarm on their faces: walking on without seeing them, yet aware nonetheless that they are staring at you: a painful burning sensation running up my back and seeming to focus itself at the nape of my neck: but going on, going on, crossing the street between the cars stopped for the traffic light, reaching the opposite side where half a dozen prostitutes are stationed night and day: walking on and on still, newspaper stands, cafeteria, a stationery store, records and school supplies, Africans peddling totems and native handcrafts, the street stalls outside a Prisunic, sidewalks crowded with people: signs of revulsion, anxiety, nausea suddenly appear on their faces, creating a vacuum round about him, surrounding him with a spectacular halo of danger: an animal of an unknown, unclassifiable species, the miserable product of an accursed astral conjunction: let us move away from him so his breath doesn't touch us, let us prudently cover our mouths and our noses with soft sterilized handkerchiefs: let us phone the city sanitation department: send the truck that picks up stray dogs, beggars, the sick, madmen, bums, drug addicts: his presence is a threat to public health: all of us run the risk of getting infected: walking down the Boulevard Sébastopol, slipping past the entrance to the Strasbourg-Saint Denis métro station, the newsstand selling Yugoslav and Turkish magazines, the little table where a man encases all sorts of documents in plastic in a matter of seconds: then coming face to face with the smiling, ever-watchful lady-witness in a felt hat, absorbed in the usual exercise of her minuscule apostolate: the distribution of little pamphlets imprinted with a sun whose rays rend the abominable bonds of sin and a message from the founder of the HEALTH AND HEALING mission: handing him a copy, with an imperturbable benevolent expression, not even noticing that I am the one there in front of her: oui, mon pauvre ami, Dieu pense à vous, Il vous veut du bien, Il se soucie de votre salut, laissez-Le donc rentrer dans votre coeur!: votre maladie peut être le péché de votre âme, mais de même qu'Il a guéri le lépreux, de même Il vous pardonnera chaque péché, si vous Lui faites appel: croyez-moi, rien n'est impossible avec le Seigneur!: a circle of curious onlookers, a crowd immediately gathering round the protagonists, popular expectation centered on the pocket of the phantasmagorical overcoat in which his hand is timidly thrust: will he take the rectangular sheet of paper that the pious activist is confidently holding out to him?: the suspense is prolonged for a few seconds: an ineffable expression on the face of the devout disciple, silence on the part of the onlookers eagerly awaiting the unpredictable reaction of this apparition: finally

9

the specter's hand hesitantly emerges, with the caution of one resurrected abandoning the shadows of the tomb: suddenly touched by grace, his hand reaches out for the sheet of paper, but the next instant he changes his mind, raises the hand in a wrathful gesture meant to overpower her utterly, it lands smack in the middle of her cheek, I give her a resounding slap in the face: ma bghit ual-lú men-nek, smaati?: and to top it off, adding, as he turns his back and elbows his way out of the stupefied crowd: naal d-din um-mék!: murmurs, surprised exclamations, fearful delayed reactions of outraged dignity: ça alors!: j'ai jamais vu une chose pareille!: ils se croient tout permis!: frapper publiquement une femme!: oh, vous savez, chez eux, je les connais bien, j'ai vécu quinze ans là-bas!: avez-vous besoin de quelque chose, Madame?: c'est rien, Monsieur, c'est rien, un pauvre malheureux, il n'est pas sain d'ésprit, on peut pas lui tenir rigueur de son geste!: safe and sound: out of reach of their voices, on the other side of the boulevard: the aquarium-terrace of the Café de France, another newspaper stand, a tailor shop selling ready-made suits, a furrier's advertising remaindered goods, the red symbol of a combined tobacco shop and café: continuing on up the Boulevard Strasbourg, paying no attention to the people staring at me: grimacing faces, expressions of disgust and loathing: my bountiful harvest: clearing out of his path with visible haste: unable to face the challenge that his existence presents: dusky, bare feet, insensitive to the rigors of the season: ragged, threadbare pants with improvised skylights at the knees: an overcoat with the collar raised to conceal a double absence: his ears, good heavens, where are his ears?: another movie theater, a triple bill advertised in bright blinking lights: À PLEINS SEXES, DÉCHAÎNEMENTS CHARNELS, LES JEUNES BAISEUSES: INTERDIT AUX MOINS DE 18 ANS: like fire, yes, like fire, faces, garments, smiles, sprinkle the whole thing with gasoline, cigarette lighter, matches, whatever, my eyes flamethrowers, destruction, trails of phosphorus, screams, human torches: on the pedestrian island of the rue de Metz: groping his way across the street: impermeable to, utterly aloof from the reaction that he invariably arouses: the cries of: look at his face!: no, no, I can't, it's too much, he turns my stomach!: maybe he's escaped from an insane asylum: they ought to stop him, call the police, take him to the nearest emergency ward!: a young man cradles his little boy's head against his breast, as though trying to protect him from your evil eye: another quickens his step and crosses himself: horror, loneliness, emptiness, the acute sensation that death is clinging to his back like glue: what's he saying?: he seems to be mumbling something: isn't there anybody who'll look after him?: to the quarantine station, to the hospital, to jail instead of contaminating our streets!: hat store, handbags and leather goods, passage de l'Industrie, the livid, sulphurous, hair-raising billboard for a horror film: L'HORRIBLE CAS DU DOCTEUR X: vampires leaning over bare breasts, sharp fangs, profuse trickles of blood: the monthly period of a nubile damsel destined to revive the appetite of a perverse Faustian researcher?: or to rejuvenate the thyroid gland of an aged châtelaine who has repaired to a remote fortified castle in the snow-covered heights of the Carpathians?: the eager expression with which the lady in question, drawn in such a way as to be mindful of the queen in Snow White, is contemplating the doctor's sucking of the breasts of the artificially sleeping virgin, obviously points to the second, more exciting hypothesis: vampirism as the fruit of a noble marital sentiment: a sentiment serving an evil cause, yet worthy of sympathy withal: focusing with a blind gaze, like a camera with a cap blocking the lens, on the bit players and props displayed on the posters outside the movie theater, above and to either side of the box office: the test tubes, bats, vivisection amphitheaters, cold storage rooms for corpses in the Transylvanian castle: with-

12

out noticing, apparently, the huge new crowd that has gathered: the sudden, dense cluster of passersby staring at him, staring at me, as though at yet another advertisement for the film: a being created by the twisted, crepuscular mind of the learned and anguished researcher: silently waiting for me to go into action: hypnotized by your tense, painful immobility: they must have put him out here as a come-on for the film: that disgusting stuff on his face is makeup and paint: nowadays they'll use any sort of gimmick, in the worst possible taste, to push whatever it is they're selling: an exaggeratedly realistic image of horror: the costume's absolutely perfect!: not seeing them, not noticing their presence, deliberately offering them an icy transparency, invisibility: eyes focused only on the fantastic proliferation in the Grand-Guignolesque movie poster: bizarre creatures with the awkward articulation of crabs: deformed women, suffering from dropsy or ominously pregnant: lucifugous monsters fleeing pell-mell an underground explosion: dismissing from his mind the real terror: taking shelter, as though in a safe place, in the merciful kingdom of illusion: mingling with the figures on the billboard that are grinning, pulling you toward them by the coattails, hopping and skipping about his bare feet, with fierce fervor making me part

13

of their creeping, crawling, slithering scenography:
walking through the outer lobby plastered with posters and photographs, gliding like a sleepwalker past
the startled elderly woman in the box office, going
down the short flight of stairs to the tiny auditorium:
turning the flashlight beam of the usherette trying to
show you to a vacant seat around to your face and
hearing her muffled scream, her stifled cry of panic as
she steps back, drops her little flashlight, turns tail,
pushes the door at the bottom of the stairs open and
rushes up the steps: back inside the womb again:
enveloped in soothing fetal shadow: temporarily
freed from the world that is his thanks to the generous, timely amnesty offered by the darkness: contemplating the grim neo-gothic great hall of the
castle made ready for the repast: the doctor and his
wife presiding over the banquet in honor of the beautiful young blonde guest: the rectangular table laden
with food, the candelabra giving forth a dim, flickering light, the attentive frozen-faced butler: his predictable gesture as he pours the fateful potion into
the victim's cut-crystal glass: the fierce, conspiratorial
glance exchanged by the host and hostess as the heedless damsel raises it to her lips and forthwith falls
unconscious, with lightning swiftness: the immediate removal of the defenseless body to the laboratory
in an adjoining room: the covetous expression on the

châtelaine's face as the scientist strips the hapless victim naked
oh, how young she is!
patience, my darling, I'm going to draw out all her
blood!
closing my eyes, resting, sleeping, being who I am,
they're not looking, the horror of the film is protecting me, the inferno, their world, has disappeared,
they're no longer paying any attention to the fact that
he exists, they've paid for their tickets, they want to
enjoy the show, a way of killing time, leaving you in
peace in the first row, forgetting the city, the streets,
the crowds, the naked aggression of the people
streaming past, journeying to other places, other set-
tings, flying through the air on a carpet, traversing
entire continents, oceans, another country, roaming
from place to place, hospitality, the nomad's way of
life, vast expanses of space, other voices, his language,
my dialect, as in the days long ago, in their midst,
alive, myself, heading, free at last, toward the market

RADIO LIBERTY

our most noble byword: progress: colonizing the distant future by subjecting it to rigorous programming: thereby sacrificing a natural propensity for indolence and game-playing: ridding ourselves, one after the other, of our atavistic customs: gradually bringing human aspirations into conformity with the enlightened imperatives of production

creating among the citizenry a solid consumer mentality: the constant invention of new necessities whose proper satisfaction obliges the individual to strive continually to improve and surpass himself:

adapting technology to man, and conversely, man to technology: fostering the symbiosis of both: devoting the totality of our physical and moral resources to the attainment of the proposed objective: our firm resolve to reach the goal we have set ourselves excludes any and every sort of concession and hence we warn our enemies and detractors: we stand ready to employ every possible means to maintain the level of consumption of the people: and should it prove necessary, to sacrifice the people themselves: this is a philosophical principle that we shall never compromise

an exciting prospect: the adaptation of the individual, step by step, to his habitat, the gradual mutation of the organism in response to new technical and environmental conditions: just as subterranean species can dispense with the sense of sight since it has become a superfluous luxury to them or as the transition from the quadruped to the biped has taken the form of a remarkable reduction and refinement of his manual extremities, so the revolution that we are undertaking will eventually produce a fabulous specimen of the new man, a distinct type of human being: the progressive atrophy of those organs that through lack of use, or to be more precise, lack of employment, become pointless and bothersome: why continue, for instance, to have extra-long and extra-strong legs if the function for which they were created is now quite superfluous?: the more and more extensive use of the private passenger car, by upsetting all our preconceived ideas about motion, has relegated our age-old skills at walking to the junk heap: hence our bold, provocative predictions: the man of tomorrow will have members perfectly adapted to the structure of the motor vehicle that he owns: forearms ideally suited to the diameter of the wheel, tibias of precisely the right length to reach the clutch pedal, brake, and accelerator: a total harmony between nature and industry: the perfect conformity of the laws of evolution of homo sapiens and the norms of production of the planning center

instilling a sense of responsibility in the minds of our citizens: helping them to see clearly within themselves: smoothing the arduous path that leads to the future by doing away with any and every obstacle standing in the way of the development and flowering of their personality: turning each individual into a total, absolute consumer who leaves in our hands not only the organization of his professional life but also the satisfaction of his every whim in the most private and intimate sphere of his existence: from the choice of wearing apparel, hair style, lighter, car, vacation trips, favorite sports, et cetera to the careful selection of his spouse and the meticulously planned parenthood of his offspring, always taking into account, of course, the particular nature of his desires and aspirations

unaffected, spontaneous, self-assured, modern man lives his life without fundamentally altering his manner of being: his well-developed sense of identity is reflected in the consistency of his style: that personalized style that is all his own, the tailor-made measure of the man himself, is the one that we offer you, having coordinated for you a series of combinations that may often appear to be bold and daring, but are unfailingly compatible: from underwear to sweaters, from mufflers to double-breasted jackets, from trousers to hats, everything will go together beautifully: a simple happenstance?: not at all!: our secret lies in recognizing your uniqueness, since we know from experience that the ego of every man differs from that of every other: it is precisely this difference, oftentimes hidden, unavowable, that we carefully cultivate: do you dream, for example, of crawling naked over a rough brick floor in obedience to the whistle of an enigmatic blonde disguised as a railway stationmaster?: do you yearn to have a fold-ing umbrella shoved up your ass, where it will open out like an ordinary umbrella?: you will be shown the means to make these fantasies and many others a concrete reality the moment you contact us: don't be satisfied any longer with the shoddy workmanship of the individual amateur handyman with an outmoded craft-mentality!: the world is changing, customs and habits vary nowadays, tastes are evolving: in our day and age a new concept of life has taken over, with a quite different scale of values: to become your real, total self call upon our services!: we will immediately point out to you your most distinctive individual trait

the most solid asset, the most dependable value: your youth
ideas associated with it: health, spontaneity, elegance, slenderness, boundless energy, self-confidence, sportiness, English tailoring, credit cards, parties, jet travel, scotch on the rocks, a redheaded mistress, a fast convertible: therefore: the need to defend it from the ravages of time: to cling discreetly but doggedly to your ephemeral graces: why look your age when the very concept of age is misleading and ambiguous?: why keep your sparse gray hair, your decayed teeth, your wrinkled and sickly looking skin if you have

within your reach the stimulating possibility of re-
placing them with a subtle and circumspect artificial
natural look?: the era of the toupee, plastic surgery,
false teeth and all the ridicule that they bring in their
wake has fortunately given way to better things:
what we offer you today is the replacement of your
epidermis, hair follicles, incisors, eyeteeth, molars un-
naturally worn away by the inevitable tensions of
modern society with new elements that will be harmoniously combined to form a completely over-
hauled, seductive image of your physical organism:
we will enable you to laugh, run, have sex, show
yourself in public without complexes, reconciling the
picture of yourself as a person that you present to
others and the one that you yourself cherish in your
heart of hearts: but we need your collaboration in
order to do so: make up your mind to be really and
truly young!: don't allow circumstances, fatigue,
your unfortunate pessimistic turn of mind to decide
for you!: just remember: delegating your power of
decision to us will always be the safest and surest way
of deciding for yourself

our two diametrically opposed poles: consumption
versus production: the suppression of intermediate
states, the elimination of those slack periods in which

citizens do not consume what they have produced and do not produce what they will later consume: hence the need to lay down strict rules and regulations for the use of leisure time, to channel the desires and aspirations of the individual by sensitizing him to the magnetic field of our social philosophy: to associate for example the idea of repose with that of soft mattresses and sleeping pills, that of wandering footloose and fancy-free with the vast gamut of possibilities of escaping it all worked out by various advertising agencies: better still: to aim at the perfect simultaneity of the two poles: the creation of a paradigm of the productive consumer and vice versa by provoking a deliberate split in his psychic and vital mechanisms and functions: the possibility of eating, drinking, driving, diverting himself without thereby abandoning his fundamental status as a link in the tremendous chain of progress: the intoxicating prospect of prolonging during sleep his duties and responsibilities carried out during work hours: a qualitative, dialectical leap with incalculable consequences: the prideful adoption on the part of the individual of a superior and nobler model of humanity

---

an evident fact: with each passing day the social gains of our era are becoming more onerous for the purse of the taxpayer overwhelmed by the heavy burden that he is forced to bear in these difficult times of crisis: does this mean that we must throw overboard what unquestionably constitutes a giant step toward the security and progress of all mankind?: can we reverse our course without openly rejecting our dogmas and giving up our optimistic beliefs in the ever-onward march of history?: the answer is obviously in the negative and any decision leading in that direction would violate our principles of free play and individual responsibility: we consider it indispensable, on the contrary, to take the bull by the horns and confront the dilemma with boldness and imagination: our proposal?: very simple: a spectacular reduction of the budget of the Welfare State by means of a superior form of consciousness-raising: instilling in pensioners, the sick, the disabled, and in all those persons in general who go to make up what the communications media euphemistically refer to as senior citizens, a clear and objective view of their miserable status as parasites: useless individuals who do not produce what they consume and who, by all the rules of elementary logic, ought to abstain from consuming: setting up radio and television courses on the subject and conditioning them gently but firmly to accept the only rational solution: their voluntary disappearance for dignity's sake: we therefore advise our viewers and radio listeners: remove yourselves from our sight when the time comes!: don't subject your loved ones unnecessarily to the detestable image of your physical and mental deterioration!: we will help you make the transition to a state of eternal repose: the expenses of the operation will naturally be borne by the public treasury and we will be honored to offer you and your family, as a bonus, a splendid, unforgettable funeral

disadvantages of the system: lack of time, the pressures of daily living: the necessity of sacrificing not only one's leisure hours, full of programmed pastimes, but also those habits and customs which, through repetition, frequently take on among those who observe them the solemn force of a ritual: the widespread belief, for instance, that it is one's duty to make love in order to ensure the perpetuation of the species: an extremely complicated ceremony, the absurd repetition of which throughout married life not only becomes a bore for the conjugal partners but also involves, from the standpoint of the community, an incalculable loss of work time!: getting undressed, fondling each other, lying together et cetera: despite the fact that other much more convenient and efficient means exist to make certain that the woman who desires a child will have an immediate, hygienic, subtle, almost ethereal pregnancy: all she need do is call upon our insemination bank, branch offices of which have been set up even in the most remote provinces: if, for whatever reason, your husband and yourself find yourselves thousands of miles apart and the situation gives every appearance of continuing for some time: if your spouse, madame, is sterile or the two of you do not have the time for trifling, or if, in a word, you find the act of procreating tedious, we offer you a solution: visit us!: the operation is performed with surprising swiftness, in absolutely aseptic and perfectly hygienic conditions: the bank protects the anonymity of the donors, but it makes a thorough study of both their personal and family traits in order to guarantee the impeccable quality of our product: for this reason, we offer a monetary incentive to males possessing a superior pedigree: their ejaculations are kept in plastic tubes at precisely the proper temperature, thus ensuring that you will not be confronted with the hideous surprise of having given birth to a half-breed child, the sad fruit of a hybrid, impure gene: our endeavor has been crowned with a success that we ourselves find truly amazing, and today the vast majority of mothers make use of our services instead of exposing themselves to the difficulties and dangers of a bothersome and pointless act of copulation

according to data gathered by our sociologists and city planners, a mysterious but demonstrable correlation exists between suicide and street violence: a dramatic increase in the latter will be accompanied by an equally spectacular decrease in the number of persons who successfully attempt to end their own lives: conversely, the greater the number of suicides, the fewer criminal assaults, murders, and other bloody misdeeds will be reported in the pages of our sensationalist press: a subtle connection which, like the law of hydraulic equilibrium, keeps the total number of victims at a constant, practically invariable level
a discovery of capital importance, from which our democratically elected municipal authorities are attempting, as is only logical, to extract the maximum possible benefit: for if the press and opposition groups might perhaps rightfully tax them with responsibility for the shocking crime rate, deeds of violence, muggings, holdups and the like that in societies less cautious than ours continually threaten citizens' lives, who would ever dream of holding

them responsible for what are beyond question pure and simple suicides?: hence, properly advised by a team of psychologists and public relations experts, we have launched a discreet and effective campaign to promote among the masses the idea of the nobility and dignity of the act whereby a person takes it upon himself, of his own free will, to end his days: from the projection of films and spot commercials in which voluntary death is depicted in kindly, almost cheery tones to omnipresent, downright obsessive advertisements for powerful sedatives and sleeping pills that are easy and painless to use: not to mention the establishment of an SOS telephone service for misfits, alcoholics, people who are severely depressed: a prerecorded message in a warm, persuasive female voice: simple bits of advice repeated at regular intervals in different languages: don't prolong your suffering needlessly!: don't allow yourself to become a burden on your family and friends!: resolve to put an end to your unbearable loneliness!: break once and for all the vicious circle of your anxiety!: your disappearance from this world need not necessarily be as unpleasant as you may think!: with a little imagination on your part it can even be delightful!: followed immediately by a complete list of drugs available without a prescription in our principal department stores and pharmacies: fraternally advising those who call in as to the proper way of taking them: one, two, three dozen pills in a glass of plain tap water, adding a few drops of whiskey to make sure it taste better: or for lofty and pure souls, incurable romantics, a bubbling glass of champagne and selections from Wagner, Chopin, and Rachmaninoff as background music: and finally, convincing those who are still hesitating by reading them specially chosen passages from Seneca or some other glorious paradigm: the epidemic of voluntary deaths that has struck the city recently has swept away all trace of violence from our horizon and put a damper on the campaign on the part of vicious malcontents and dissenters enternally opposed to the energetic and ingenious policies pursued by our provident municipal management

equally undeniable: the existence of certain dark spots in the overall picture: isolated, recalcitrant nuclei, incapable of grasping the underlying assumptions and of profiting from the advantages of our incomparable consumption-oriented system: deliberately remaining aloof from the great maelstrom of change: communities of dubious origin, stubbornly clinging to anachronistic standards of living that have been rendered totally obsolete thanks to our rapid rate of progress: parasitic groups, the waste

products of social metabolism, whose pathetic inability to adapt to the society of well-being they de-
ceptively pass off, when playing to the gallery, as a
gesture of rejection

in its sensational exclusive program, Journey to the
Center of the Earth, PB News has filmed these
shadowy individuals for you, crouching in their lair
three hundred feet below ground!: a rudimentary but
resistant community of moles who, eschewing our
principles of industriousness and high productivity,
are building in the perpetual gloom of the catacombs
an atavistic, ahistorical, atemporal social structure in
which the solar cycle, the basis of the calendar of all
known civilizations to date, plays no role whatsoever!: our troglodytes have preferred darkness to
light, filth to cleanliness, the rodent to the human, a
difficult choice to understand, ladies and gentlemen,
but one which our special team from PB News, roving reporters Joe Brown and Ben Hughes, will try to
find a plausible explanation for tonight at nine on the
dot, with the help of the very individuals in question!

ANGEL

the true story of my life?: an incurable trauma suf-
fered in my youth: a single, violent, obsessive image,
quite enough to leave me with no appetite and unable to sleep if, like the ordinary run of mortals, I
were subject night and day to such petty, vulgar necessities: a primal scene, a continually repeated point
of reference that haunts you, has haunted you, and
will haunt you: a ceaseless beginning all over again,
one step forward and two back, with my Sisyphus-
rock on my back: how to defuse, pray tell, the tension
of that extremely painful episode?: I have tried, you

30

have tried medicines prescribed by doctors, the traditional remedies of faith healers, to no avail: potions, infusions, syrups, cold compresses, herbs, unguents, vials of salts: absorbing, intense effort, or on the contrary dolce far niente, long periods of rest and relaxation: but zero results, my love, absolutely zero: everything the same, exactly the same, as in the beginning: thalassotherapy in Brittany, taking the waters in Sidi Harassam, autocriticism meetings in Party cells, lying supine on a psychiatrist's velvety couch: or else tripping, getting stoned, getting high: acting as though I were a frivolous creature without a care in the world: comporting myself in a deliberately childish, shocking manner: visiting the doctor's office without a brassiere, winking suggestively when the nurse left the room, insisting on his unhooking your garterbelt, pretending to fall into a faint when he examined me: and the whole thing ending up exactly where it started, stuck in the same place as before: a disaster, my love: utter despair: witchcraft and philters and spiritualist seances with mediums, black cats, tables set to dancing, all to no avail: no longer able to do your job properly: in a word: a hopeless case: everything up there bored me: the tiresome paternalistic atmosphere, the servile zeal of your colleagues, the intolerable slavery of the daily schedule: plenitude become emptiness, perfection an oppressive, stifling state: you began to neglect duties and rites, yawned loudly during services, interrupted meetings and ceremonies with brusque falsettos, expansive, extremely contagious bursts of laughter: and your bad example spread, threatened to destroy group discipline, and more serious still, to undermine the efficacy and solidity of the basic statutes themselves: your sacred, common cultural values, the intangible, imperishable legacy of the Father: no other recourse remained save to bring me before a Court of Conduct: you were unmoved by counsel and exhortations, promises of leniency and forgiveness, subtle pressures, threats: I stood firm: the beatific dwelling of her peers didn't suit her at all: she unburdened her conscience, you set forth the reasons for your straying from the straight and narrow path, I brought up the extraordinary incidents that had occurred during the mission with which we were entrusted: the visit to the home of the just man, the crowd's envious gaze, laying siege to the house as ordered: how to resign myself after that to the immutable routine of a monotonous, rigid system with rules and regulations for everything, down to the very last detail?: to the uniform expression, smiling and ethereal, of comrades who fulfilled the goals assigned, repeated the slogans, tirelessly sang the praises of the Leader in person, like trained parrots?: their childishness and dependency set my nerves on edge, their docile acceptance of the nepotism of the all-powerful head of the Secretariat and their willingness to obey her slightest whim thoroughly irritated and disheartened her: they were prepared to do anything so long as it was in accordance with the party line: to deny proven fact if that were necessary: credo quia absurdum: to call what they could see was white black: but such a state of affairs couldn't go on: the meetings of the rank-and-file provided for in the rules turned into an empty ritual, reduced to the monotonous chanting of a few soporific slogans or pointless polite parlor-prattle with the favorites and the relatives of the self-titled Intercessoress and Mediatrix of All Graces: I tried, to no avail, to provoke discussion, to restore the original purity of our principles, to scrape the mold off the words in our vocabulary: in vain she pointed to, you pointed to the deviationist practices that had insidiously interfered with the harmonious development of the community: bureaucratic inertia, lack of spontaneity, depoliticization of the rank-and-file, strict censorship, the distinction between leaders and followers, the arrogance of the former, the total helplessness of the lower echelons in the face of their supposed representatives, the fact that members of the nine hierarchies could not be removed from office, the absence of forums for discussion, the intrigues and

33

maneuvers of coteries, the omnivorous concentration of all power in the remote apex of the pyramid: they did not listen to you: clinging to a literal and opportunistic interpretation of doctrine, immured in their privileges as though in an impregnable bulwark they turned a deaf ear, ignored my arguments, pointed their finger at what they called errors and personal attitudes incompatible with the dignity and nobility of my office: instead of fruitful discussions, bold and innovative proposals, a veritable hailstorm of petty accusations: indolence, moral laxity, overestimation of the importance of my own role, subjectivism, the desire for stardom: with the tendency toward compulsive hysteria inherent in every witchhunt: surrounded on every hand by the mistrust and ill-will of her comrades, kept under constant surveillance, trailed, her every act, movement, word, no matter how trivial, subjected to the closest scrutiny: gossip-mongering, the oppressive atmosphere of a spy-scare, psychotic fears of a vast plot afoot, defensive paranoia, a police mentality: tricky questions, cutting, contemptuous remarks, threatening looks, informers: continually adding new bits of evidence to the ridiculous indictment they were drawing up against her: that I fell asleep during the Leader's speeches, recited the canonical prayers reluctantly and dispiritedly, tuned in on clandestine foreign radio broadcasts, was captivated by the fashion magazines that she read in secret: grotesque accusations of cosmopolitanism, base, vile, and despicable imitation of harmful, bizarre, alien manners and morals: or pure and simple fabrications dreamed up by one or another frenetic, sectarian, brainwashed activist: the supposed fact, for instance, that on singing the Fiat Lux I had added "And likewise Volkswagen," malicious calumny that was passed on in whispers till it finally reached the shocked ears of the Mother's brain trust: accusations of irreverence and disrespect, failure to keep my vows, grave infractions of discipline: impossible to channel the debate in such a way as to permit orderly and reasonable discussion: my militant sisters hurled accusations at me and reproached me at the top of their lungs, used the confused statements of my hapless companion to suit their own purposes, sought a scapegoat for their own hidden anxieties and secret frustrations: but it was quite evident that they were dying of envy: jealous of your difficult but exciting mission: of the trust placed in you: of the fact that you had been given preference over the daughters of the just man by the evil and perverted inhabitants: a sentiment that was quite obvious beneath the thin veneer of feigned indifference with which they observed the behavior of the women of that uncouth and vulgar universe: whispered conversations on the subject of the prominence of their breasts, the firm fullness of their hips, the genesic arcanum of their hidden hollows and crevices: how many times, behind the backs of the hierarchs and leaders, you had surprised them adjusting the folds of their tunics, measuring, with the aid of a dressmaker's tape, the tiny perimeter of their waists!: they were fascinated, I swear, by their saucy, provocative co-quettishness, the incredible ease with which they sur-rendered to the unbridled appetites of the males: those brief and fierce couplings about which they spoke with cautious and circumspect prudery, cloak-ing themselves in a mantle of majestic disdain and modesty: what, they said to each other, could that feminine organ—often imagined but never seen, though all of you intuited that it must be pearly, floral, exquisite, like the fragrant perianth of a plant—be like?: can it be pretty, receptive, sensitive, delicate, sweet-smelling?: en petit comité we debated its possi-ble capabilities of expansion, its marvelous powers of dilation: since what hangs between the legs of you men, my love, was an old story, so to speak: once their intelligence-gathering mission was com-pleted, the envoys were in the habit of slipping sketches made from different angles into their valises: these then circulated clandestinely from one group to another, with neither import license nor customs stamp: in short: rather than holding women in contempt we were secretly jealous of them: and so you, she, despite having a smooth-contoured, unadorned body, shorn hair, an asexual face, had been chosen in preference to the flowering shoots of the sacrosanct male by that nucleus of inveterate connoisseurs: enough to cause the milit-aunties of the organization to gnash their teeth, from the inferior choirs to the most exalted hierarchies: why her, me, and not us, that is to say them, they asked themselves, do you follow me, my love?: green with envy, from secretaries of cells to heads of sections, asking over and over, harping on the subject: what did they do, come on, tell us, you slut, out with it, did they couple with you, feel you up, show you their privates?: and she, I, still traumatized by the importuning, the screaming and shouting, the embarrassment of the host, the morbid curiosity of his late wife, the hurt expression of the daughters, the earnest pleas, the weeping, the threats: haunted by the image of those bold, hirsute, savage brutes, overcome with violent desires to subject me and my thoroughly distressed colleague to the spasms of a wild, fierce pleasure that we knew nothing of: I was unable, she was unable to adapt herself to the parameters of a normal existence, to endure the ill-will of her humiliated comrades: the trial before the Court of Conduct was a relief for you:

37

the recent Council had happily put an end to the excesses committed in previous periods, during the so-called personality cult, the hostile menopause of the Mother: the work camps of Avernus are now almost empty, as the Supreme Guide says in the new, expurgated version of his Writings, nobody is eliminated these days: she accepted, you accepted the irreversible verdict: guilty: and I clutched the ticket, the passport, the exit permit from my gray and wingless paradise with a feeling of having been reborn and newly baptized that anyone who knows nothing of such a experience can scarcely imagine: the outer darkness beyond eden, the tempestuous free world into which they had hurled me were for you, for her the promise and symbol of a foreseen corporal felicity, of a fruitful, stimulating derangement of the senses: the first contact with the feverish hustle and bustle of cities, the whirlwind pace of life in metropolises overwhelmed me: you frequented cabarets and nightclubs, saunas, porno shops, massage parlors: a logical reaction against the austere and monastic regime under which you had lived: it was the result of a burning thirst to know, a noble, wholesome desire to become acquainted with the facts: hard-core films in a filthy establishment on Forty-second Street, amatory instruments and gadgets and contraptions in a shop on Christopher Street for a specialized clientele: elec-

tric vibrators, studded collars and bracelets, rubber
fingers, nipple-pincers, testicular and phallic rings,
shackles, gags, handcuffs, whips, harnesses, leather
straps: confused, perplexed, stupefied by the incredible collection of dildos of awesome sizes and dimensions: now that I know the score, things are different:
but at that time, my love, I swear to you: night after
night of doubt and anguish, holed up in her dingy,
miserable cheap hotel room, turning the subject over
and over in her mind: without managing to distin-
guish sick, dazzling fantasy from vulgar, prosaic reality: wavering between one extreme and the other
with the endlessly repeated question: Lord, Lord,
where does the truth lie?: you were forced to make
the qualitative leap, to pass from the realm of pure
speculation to exultant, concrete praxis: whereupon
she encountered insurmountable obstacles: her mini-
mal body, adapted to the subtle conditions peculiar
to ether, lacked organs suitable for fecundation, save
for a poetic and highly improbable pollination: she
was obliged to have an operation, to have a deep
incision made in your smooth pubis and a soft, warm,
hospitable receptacle created, in which the instrument could comfortably expand and easily reach the
limits of an extreme and concise rigor: I had con-
sultations with famous specialists, she explained her
case to psychiatrists and doctors, sampled the first

fruits of a generous hormone treatment: she laid aside, you laid aside your severe, functional habit and took to wearing daring, provocative, tight-fitting garments emphasizing the enticing convexities of your new and opulent configuration: without yet daring to take the plunge, to face up to the challenge, she militated, you militated in marginal, hyperpolitical, metasexist, ultraradical minority groups: she claimed the right to be different, to fulfill yourself by accepting your enriching anomaly, to live publicly, in the full light of day, according to the dictates of my inescapable singularity: she took part in meetings and marches, sit-ins and lockouts, I offered my services as an experienced organizer to various splinter groups, I became a shock trooper of different avant-garde movements: after a certain time however, not being an innocent kid after all, she began to see covert signs of the same defects and flaws as in the supposed Jehovan paradise: dogmatism, will to power, doctrinal sclerosis, compartmentalization, isolation, the surreptitious reestablishment of hierarchies: you pointed out the dangers, she denounced the emergence of a new elite class of leaders, the sole result of which was to bring upon herself a total lack of understanding, rancor, venomous hatred on the part of the others: accused once again of petty-bourgeois subjectivism and egotism, the violation of rules and regulations, subversion, deviationism of every kind, sort, and degree: of complacently splashing about in the muddy waters of inexcusable theoretical lacunae: proscribed once more, excluded from councils and conclaves, the victim of all manner of vicious slander, a leper, a plague carrier, a source of contamination: in a word: deep depression: the usual cycle of tranquilizers, sleeping pills, amphetamines: the tearful rehearsal of complaints and laments: vague thoughts of suicide: alienation from the industrial world, its gigantic manipulation of human beings and material goods stood out in my mind with a clarity that was my salvation: dildos, the bizarre collection of metal and leather contraptions were of no avail if, when the moment of truth arrived, the inevitable confrontation of H-hour, homo faber exhibited in the arena a remorseful, timid, pitiful, retractile peduncle: I was forced to flee from such surroundings, run the risk of undergoing a complex, intricate operation, try my luck in rugged, remote precincts: the setting of a romantic film of yesteryear was the ideal background against which the protagonists of my frustrated rape of long ago could harmoniously play their assigned roles: upright men such as yourself, possessed of immediate, powerful sex appeal, armed with a superb, unique, inescapable tool: I hastened, I ran, I flew, she crossed the ocean, traversed the lofty mountain range, reached

41

the plain: a renowned surgeon laid out a flower-filled garden for you, an inviting, delightful, pleasant place in which the intense, pent-up fervor of a Bedouin might tame her age-old, atavistic urges: the rest of the story you already know, my love: the long-postponed realization of the dream conceived in the confines of the accursed, obliterated city: hitching yourself to the yoke, joining the horde of camp followers and harlots trailing along in the wake of the Moroccan infantrymen and soldiers of the Legion, throwing away your useless high-heeled shoes, sinking your bare feet into the delicate ripples of the sand dunes, walking on and on, losing myself in the desert

SEASIDE CEMETERY

slowly, slowly, amid the deafening din of the highway, to the dense little grove of trees beneath which, good heavens, it's him, he's here, he's come back, where?: I swear it, haven't you seen him?: those traveling on foot often take cover there to protect themselves from the sun's stubborn onslaught, looking at him, looking at me, with barely discernible signs of happiness, surprised, discreet friendly gestures, a joyous recognition scene after such a long absence, as if by going away, by leaving them, I had subtly deprived them of something, there they are, my women

43

friends, there they are, your men friends, not daring to stop him and greet him to his face, murmuring, whispering, with visible jubilation: yes, it's true, it's been a long time, it seems like only yesterday, incredible, as good-looking as ever, you haven't changed, he hasn't changed: young boys, young girls, nubile bodies hinted at beneath caftans, stout, mature women, incognito, dark glasses, simple face veils, white kerchiefs bound tightly round their heads: vendors hawking lottery tickets and cigarettes sold one by one, shoeshine boys squatting on their haunches, soldiers: red and green berets, stripes, shoulder braid, loitering, cruising, happy, holding hands: messenger boys, horse traders, beggars, bourgeois, snow-white fesí robes, traffic cops with bushy mustaches, soliloquists babbling away in mad fury, cripples, kids, foreigners: boots, billy clubs, belt, leather chest straps of a pair from the Auxiliary Forces: at the intersection of the main streets of the city, beyond the taxi stands where crowds of people are always waiting: submerged now in the current of customers from the market close by: through the arcade to the left, past the pharmacy and the police booth, the shaded terrace of the café, the dummy in chef's costume holding up the menu outside the Doghmi restaurant: dodging itinerant peddlers displaying their meager portable wares: socks pants shirts female undergarments nail clippers scissors garish color prints medicinal herbs: prepared to cause all of it to disappear from sight with a flick of the wrist and swiftly take off with it at the least sign or threat of danger: a hasty exodus down narrow little side streets, then patiently biding their time until the sun comes out again: wisely waiting with the caution born of long experience for the passing squall to end, as unexpectedly as it began: a scene repeated daily from one end of the familiar itinerary to the other: escorted by the mute respect of his admirers: happy to have him among us once again, to realize that neither distance nor the years have taken him away from us forever, still our brother, as in the good old days when he performed here in these very streets: exhibitions of.strength and skill, an incomparable command of the spoken word, recitations from the Koran: laughing till tears came to our eyes at his bawdy stories, his sudden guffaws, the graphic, sly, cunning gestures with which he drew crowds around him like a magnet, as young and self-assured as ever, still good-looking despite the liberating lopping-off of his useless, bothersome ears, happy to find myself among them once again, to note with pride that they haven't forgotten me: there's nobody like you: I had only to install myself on the sidewalk, invoke heaven's mercy, cross my arms, let loose the impetuous flood of your words to bring them flocking around him, capture their attention, keep them quiet, enthralled, in suspense, inhabitants of a pure and perfect world, as clear as an algebraic proof: greetings, handshakes, kisses, compliments, smiles, all the girls are watching me: as he turns down the street that is a continuation of Mohamed-el-Jamís, past the peddlers of old clothes lined up in front of the Chamal restaurant, taking care not to bump into pedestrians coming out of the dry goods store, the kids lined up outside the Mauritania movie theater: walking along as though in a dream, blinded by the dazzling reflections of whitewashed buildings and walls, Moorish troops on leave, cruising epheboi, women fresh from the hammam, hands and feet carefully dyed with henna: passing by the Restaurant de l'Union, the mataam-el-Jurría, the derb Sebbahi: with footsteps as supple and stealthy as those of a Bedouin suitor: as if you were still just twenty years old and awaiting a chance to display your talents, your sermons, your jokes, a faithful audience that never disappoints you: tense, fervent young faces, a dense crowd gathered round you, a shower of coins, applause, handkissing, freedom of the will, your voice recovered, lord and master of your own life, in the quiet streets of the medina that witnessed your past triumphs, a refuge lending itself to a thousand and one love duels: carpets, sheepskins, goatskins, clean, firm, smooth bodies, a vernal flowering of nipples, narrow, moist slits, innocent, timid kisses, peals of pure, sparkling, spontaneous, throaty laughter: feeling the tumular rush of blood, the dong's obdurate rebellion against its own oppressive weight, the vertical defiance of supposedly infallible laws: a telegraphic code of winks, anxious blushes behind clouds of veils, rapid signs at a distance arranging a hypothetical rendezvous: leaps and bounds of caged wild animals, a pulsating climax on a fleeceless pubis, hips that ripple like dunes, a graceful body willingly yielding: past the display of faded lengths of cloth in the window of a Tailleur Chic and the gleaming shop sign of Au Coin de la Mode, barbershops, dry goods stores, heat relieved by an occasional breath of wind, the proximity of the sea perceptible in the dampness of whitewashed plaster walls: deserted streets and intersections, as within some drowsy Portuguese city: vestiges of fleeting and uncertain glory, front doors boarded up, rows of empty balconies, baronial mansions abandoned without compunction, victims of the negligence and ennui of owners who have come down in the world: derb Tadja, derb Midelt, derb Sidi Ahmed Ben Alí, recognition, homage, respects, it's him, it's me, it's you, obviously overjoyed to have you back, amazed at his miraculous youth, your cleverness as a jester, your skill as a bard: forgetting asepsis, coldness, anonymity, disapproving faces, hostile looks: love, freedom, adventure, aimless strolls along the streets, excitement, feeling as though you were floating on air: as you leave behind you a Tailleur Diplômé de Paris, the Coiffeur des Amants, a symbolic Tailleur de Choix: your eardrums assailed by the piercing music pouring forth from a transistor radio, an aggressive melody by Djil Djilala: you're here at last, we thought you were dead, or worse still, strayed from the fold, a stranger to your law and your blood, now we know that that's not true, you've come back, you haven't forgotten us, stay here in your own country, we'll find you a wife to serve you and keep you company, there are young girls and boys who desire you, you'll choose at your leisure the one that pleases you most: the street open before you, the crossing of the Red Sea, the contained fury of the vertical wall of water: carpenters, weavers, cabinetmakers, minstrels: two old men on their way to the mosque, a youngster with the countenance of Bruce Lee stenciled on the back of his shirt: purified by the salty caress of the wind, anointed by the diffused, transparent brightness of the air: as in the days when, once his exhibition was ended, you thrust the little sack of coins in your belt, lowered the hood of your djellabah over your eyebrows, hastened to the warm den where some girl or boy awaited me to make love: passing by the

Tailleur des Quatre Saisons, exchanging greetings with an effusive veiled woman, refusing the honeyed invitation of a Hindu film, dodging round a spectacular poster advertising kung fu, avoiding tripping over two men squatting on their haunches absorbed in a silent game of checkers: on and on, yalah, yalah, up the gentle slope that leads to the road to Slá, the gloomy fortress where they stack up prisoners, the mirador and the gardens of the castle: a little boy kisses his hand as a sign of respect, someone says God bless you, turns around, seems to follow in my footsteps: at the very last intersection where Mohamed-el-Jamís ends: trucks, cars, heavily loaded carts: the hustle and bustle of street vendors on the sidewalks, balconies, old wooden jalousies, the faded sign of the Hotel Darma: a crowd of youngsters at the entrance to the movie theater, the sudden diaspora at the end of a double feature, karate feats plus a Hindustani elixir of love: cautiously crossing the thoroughfare, heading straight through derb el Ubira: chessboards traced with chalk, little pebbles for chesspieces, onlookers standing in a circle around Spassky's amateur emulators: empty space, a soft blue sky, little clouds drifting like raveled threads of foam, bundles of hemp ready for spinning: on the slope where people used to crowd round to listen to you, traditional tales and stories dating back to your childhood, tending flocks

49

in the untilled fields and dry ravines of Tafilelt, evenings with the whole family gathered around the candle in the tent: two guards on duty in their little wooden sentry boxes, spindly palm trees, a rusted iron fence, cars with green license plates, chauffeurs and soldiers idling about, the massive building housing the Permanent Tribunal of the Armed Forces: up to the opening in the wall of the cemetery at the very top of the slope: a queue of women in front of the fountain, dipping earthen jars and pitchers in the stone basin: dramatic recognition scenes, demonstrations of fondness and affection, blessings, congratulations, compliments, suras: on the other side at last: through the narrow aperture that serves as a gateway: exposed to the freshening wind, the subtle friction of its salty, intermittent gusts: zigzagging amid anonymous tombs, gravestones, mosaic steles: threading your way through young men, girls, family groups loaded down with bundles and baskets, all set to enjoy an outing in the countryside, their day off on Friday, a picnic on the beach: a dead city with a few breaths of life left, Eros and Thanatos intermingled: nocturnal forays of soldiers and epheboi, wild transvestites on the prowl: panting, whispering, furtive caresses: the slow spasms of coupled bodies: images, memories that suddenly surface at various forks in the path: here I loved, he loved, you loved, long-vanished faces of young boys and girls, the rough ground cushioned by the folds of a heavy Saharaui burnoose: spying once again the vast panorama of the ocean, the charge of wave after wave of white steeds, sea horses that run aground on the rugged coastline: rocks, headlands, inlets, breakwaters of cement and stone, the naked lighthouse promontory: an area walled off by the thousands of gravestones aligned in roughly symmetrical rows all along the steep cliffside: up to the empty field in which children are peacefully playing soccer above graves that have weathered away, amid traces of crumbling bones: following the line of wayfarers filing along in the shadow of the wall of the Tribunal, contemplating the banners and standards of a religious brotherhood on a pilgrimage, turning off onto the shortcut used by the bathers, walking toward your right up to the rough fortress-jail: ungraspable visions, fleeting images, blurred by sun and mist: sea spray, cupolas of ruined shrines, pennants in the wind, plumed crests of palm trees, tiny women scattered amid tombs like a flight of frightened doves: presences summoned up from a time past that is continually reborn: festive visits with your parents to the hermitage of a holy man: a ride on horseback, dressed in a white caftan, on the day that you were circumcised: a sudden snip of the barber's scissors, cries of pain and jubilation, convulsions, women shrieking, blood-soaked rags: later, much later, back to the hermitage, with my new djellabah and the turban of Rissani silk patiently coiled round your head like a serpent about to strike: an insatiable thirst for life, a snail with your house on your back, sleeping in the night air or in a featherbed, depending on the whim of fate: consoler of widows, protector of young lads, comforter of troubled women: proud of my strength and eloquence, the offensive ease with which you accumulate coins and prodigally spend them in the intoxication of love-adventures or the mild euphoria of kif: feeling the youthful weight of his cock between his legs, his quickening pulse when he spies his prey, I am, you are, he is the best, the most handsome, the strongest, the cleverest: roaming among parallel lines of tombs, over trackless stretches of rough ground, along shortcuts overgrown with grass, the prayers of a woman muffled in a modest veil, cool, bracing air, a slight, salty fog with a diffuse, sfumato brightness: entering the vast, intimate makbara: an unreal unfurling of flags and pennants, processions of religious brotherhoods and mourners, the foreseeable uneasiness of bathers: a crescendo of pilgrims round the hermitage, a human river hemmed in on the cliffside, an impetuous suicidal attack on the loneliness of the lighthouse: following as best you can, almost blindly, the path traced by your restless footsteps: the objective of countless solitary walks, in search of the excitement surrounding my street exhibitions or the delicious surfeit of a sleepless night: attracted, as you know, by the mysterious silhouette bending over one of the tombs, apparently absorbed in some sort of arduous exercise in meditation: a woman or a damsel clad in a sumptuous embroidered caftan, her head covered with a silk kerchief, and carrying an exquisite Hermès bag open to the gullet, whose miscellaneous treasures she is indiscreetly inventorying: lipsticks, face creams, eyeliner, vials of perfume, foundation makeup: balls of cotton, an ostentatious jar of vaseline, mint-scented paper handkerchiefs, a package of sanitary napkins: frontal hemispheres hinting at tumescence, provocative, erectile nipples, a deep, disturbingly available hollow below her belly: the greedy fullness of her lips shows through her veil, her eyes drill into you like point-blank pistol shots: eyelashes loaded with mascara, a simple beauty mark on her cheekbone, a stirring, throaty voice, a romantic interpretation of Morocco you're here at last, I've been waiting for you for a long time, hours days weeks months years, I knew you'd make your way here, come back to me, to the exact spot where we first met, let us make love to each other as though we were possessed, it doesn't matter that others are looking, we will warm the bones in the tombs, we will make them die of sheer envy, the entire makbara is ours, we will set it on fire, it will burn with us, it will perish, we will perish, convulsed, consumed

SIC TRANSIT GLORIA MUNDI

a queen bee in the radiating center of the hive: or, to
be more precise, a tireless wingless worker reconciled
to the cramped dimensions of her alveolus: a little
cell a cavity a receptacle modestly illuminated by an
overhead light which, suspended over the tiny roof-
less compartments, overlooks wrinkles, folds, crow's-
feet, commutes sentences of twenty and thirty years,
generously grants amnesty for forced labor at delicate
dermal rejuvenation: as the drone idly or. hurriedly
makes its rounds, peeks in at the little doors standing
ajar, checks, compares, before making up its mind

55

which diligent worker it will assign, with lofty disdain, with rude and unsociable taciturnity, the task of extracting its thick, viscous, nutritive substance

here I am, my love, awaiting your arrival, full of hope and active even after all this time, paying no attention to the malice and rancor of her co-workers

regarde-moi ça, elle est encore ici, q'uest-ce qu'elle fout la gardienne, crois-tu que les mecs sont aveugles?

jeers, insulting gestures, hysterical laughter, envy, sheer envy, of me, of you, of our love, the unbreakable tie that unites the two of you, transcending space, untouched by the ravages of time: of my having been the favorite, chosen and blessed among women, an act of grace, a gift, a celestial preference that encourages and sustains her, aids her in getting round difficulties and obstacles, poverty, lack of understanding, mean-spirited spitefulness: tirelessly following in your footsteps, devoted to his worship alone, a battle-hardened combatant, a soldier-nun: ever on the alert

alors tu nous laisses la place?

don't get angry, my love: it isn't worth it

tu ferais mieux de prendre ta retraite!

see?: they're going away, or rather they've gotten tired of the whole thing, my steely disposition, my haughty indifference to their pettiness, their hostile, senile petulance confuses them: they don't know the first thing about life, they don't know that love is a delicate plant deserving to be pampered and carefully handled, fidelity perseverance exhausting efforts of memory to keep you alive, to prevent your image from being erased, eaten away by others, unable to speak, without a face or a profile, little by little become fuzzy and blurred: that's why I talk to you, dust off long-ago incidents, memories of a luminous past, moments of happiness and fulfillment, an exhilarating journey in common, bringing us closer to each other the farther we wandered apart

eh, toi, la vieille, pose bien ta perruque, tu ne vois pas qu'elle dégringole?

and you: merci

with the dignified and decorous air of a lady to the manner born, serene and intimately aware of the ephemeral nature of all worldly glories and epic endeavors

I can still see you, see myself, loitering about in front of the barracks, assailed by the compelling gaze of the Spahis, a wee bit high on the many friendly drinks downed in the bar of the hotel, euphoric, but not drunk

where?

in Bel Abbés, possibly, a one-story building next to

the Legion barracks, a patio with a minuscule swimming pool or a grandiose ornamental basin with no water in it, filled one day by you or some other husky male, massive legs spread apart, stout arms akimbo, a jubilant emptying of your kidneys, a prodigal, precisely aimed arching stream, barley fermented with hops and box, a blond, recycled spouting
you're mistaken, it wasn't in Bel Abbés
ah, yes, I remember, Khenifra, the Grand Hotel, a patio with checkered tiles, orange and lemon trees, rooms by the hour, rows of brown or green doors, a tricolored flag waving in the breeze, soldiers continually filing in and out
clad in a thin, filmy dress, delicate Holland lace, a wide satin belt, a little shoulder cape edged in silk
what's that you say?
plutôt un voile moucheté en polyester, un léger volant de dentelle qui souligne l'effet d'empiècement du corsage, le décolleté, le bas des manches et la taille: une jupe très ample à peine plongeante, coiffe et bouquet de muguet et de roses
dis donc, qu'est-ce que tu marmonnes?
don't mind them, my love, don't pay any attention: they'd like to take you away from me, dim my memories, obliterate your splendid presence, wipe you off the face of the earth, reduce you to ashes: they're envious of my experience, the wondrously solid ties

between us, my stubborn worship of you as though
you were God himself: I'm going on with my story,
you're going on, where were we?
in the Grand Hotel
ah, yes, I first saw you there, I picked you up there,
you bowled me over, tall dark, robust, radiant, your
incredible handsomeness set off to perfection by your
impeccable Spahi uniform
Spahi uniform?
perhaps that of the regiment of native sharpshooters:
boots, leather chest belt, stripes, a badge with your
ID number, balloon pants, a beret with a tassel, a
resplendent bulging fly: you said bonjour to me, that
was the only word you knew in French, and your
name: M'Hamed, Ahmed, or Mohamed: you expressed yourself melodiously in your own language
and I hung on your every word, drinking in every last
one of them like a magic potion
no, that wasn't how it was at all
I picked you up on the street, you followed me at a
few yards' distance to keep people's tongues from
wagging, with each step I took I turned around to
look at you, fearing that you'd vanish from my sight
at any moment, that I was the victim of a cruel illusion, for I was not yet persuaded of the tangible reality of this miracle
then, once I had assured myself that you actually

existed, a creature of flesh and blood, the goal of my obscure quest, the very incarnation of my atavistic ideal, I prolonged my delectable sense of anticipation, invented roundabout paths and detours, traced zig-zags and labyrinths, postponed with exquisite pain the hour when I would surrender to your embrace

pursued by the hostile stares of those on the street, belligerent men, veiled women, precocious, per-turbed youngsters: nonetheless unhurriedly strolling in the bloody light of the setting sun, round and round the rose-ocher walls

walls?

yes, walls, that wasn't a slip of the tongue, my love, the city was surrounded by walls, I first met you, we picked each other up, in Tarudant, I dressed as a Rus-sian Czarina, with a fur toque and muff like the Grand Duchess Anastasia's: I did my best to pass unnoticed, but to no avail: in that secret and passion-ate native quarter, my presence polarized vague, un-focused desires, attracted covetous glances, gave rise to hoarse, fortunately inaudible, remarks

I was staying at the time, do you remember?, in the hotel with all the flowers: my room opened onto the second-floor terrace covered with overhanging bou-gainvillea, honeysuckle, jasmine, agile species of climbing vines: an explosion in slow motion of red,

yellow, white petals to which lovely, delicate dewdrops stubbornly clung as though enraptured

from the shadowed patio, in whose slightly sunken
square center bamboos, banana trees, and other exotic
plants put forth a profusion of huge, thick, perennial
leaves with the suspect consistency of some sort of
plastic material, there came the strident voices of
hotel guests enjoying the fresh air, at tables placed
against the low wall providently surrounding the
idyllic garden: an intimate and peaceful atmosphere,
a dizzying consumption of beer beneath the implacable gaze of the owner of the hotel, capable of detect-
ing a heedless drunk instantly and obliging him to
leave, to abandon the garden's paradisiac delights,
with one simple threatening gesture of her curled
index finger

toi, fous-moi le camp!

the buzzing of a nest of wasps, the hum of bees
that you, I, my love, were vaguely aware of in
the background as I laid out various gala cos-
tumes, inventoried the treasures of my wardrobe, ex-
perimented with different lotions and moisturizing
creams, applied an attractive beauty mark to my
cheekbone

regardez-moi la Doyenne! elle parle toute seule!

seule?: la seule c'est bien toi, ma pauvre fille!: I'm

never by myself: I'm with him every minute of the day and night, I escort him, I dog his every footstep I'm with you, are you listening to what I'm saying? where were we?

ah yes, Tarudant, my room, my wardrobe, the place with all the flowers: it was just getting dark, do you remember?: after the suffocating heat of the day a soft, restorative, fragrant breeze: I am wearing an evening gown: une charmate robe en coton blanc imprimée de fleurettes à décolleté bateau: I have tied a silk kerchief round my head and covered my face with a transparent, attractive veil, as though I were a Moslem woman

she waited until the dark shadows gathered before making her appearance: as you descended the staircase you fluttered your fan before your face with a queen's genteel decorum and reserve: the patio was full of husky young lads: peasants, shopkeepers, horse traders, soldiers, policemen: a promiscuous atmosphere charged with an electrifying, sinuous eroticism: conversations were abruptly broken off: you were riddled by the piercing gaze of dark, tense faces, with burning, feline, penetrating pupils: the reality manifested itself with the rigor and clarity of an axiom: they all had erections

you crossed this eden half fainting: rejecting this setting as one not befitting her apotheosis: overtures, marks of respect, compliments, smiles, invitations, homages: haughty, triumphant, acclaimed the people's choice yet vaguely awaiting something: and there you were, my love, in your uniform of a Zouave or a dragoon, with your stern and inscrutable face, sculpted with violent hammer blows: my gaze instinctively strayed to the crotch of your heavy green trousers: despite the wretched oppression of the cloth, it was displaying obvious signs of rebellion: mirabile visu: the argument you marshaled was convincing, devastating, overwhelming!

he had, you had a slash mark or a scar on your cheek and you said your name was Abdelli, Abdellah, or perhaps Abdelhadi: look, I still have your photograph

turning her purse upside down in the dim light of the cellar: the cryptic locale of her tireless apostolate: paying no attention to the malicious gossip of the other attendants whose lives, like hers, are devoted to the relieving and removal of surplus honeyed discharges: laborious workers in their narrow, cramped little cells

no, it's not him, it isn't you, it doesn't matter, I can visualize you perfectly: I paraded in front of you with my plumes, fans, tiaras, sequins, bracelets, necklaces:

the object of the unanimous ardor of your buddies:
captivated by your gifts as an artist, her cabaret enter-
tainer's elegance and bold self-assurance
your name is Omar
the drones come and go, maintain the necessary rigid
discipline by dint of repeated manipulations, stop to
peer inside the cells, watch her, walk on, gratuitously
hand over their honey to some novice worker
alors tu ne veux pas?: tant pis pour toi!
I am, we were in Tarudant: dazzled by your imposing
bearing, my love: singing the Magnificat, reciting my
Hosanna: I winked at you with the slow solemnity of
the portrait photographer tripping the shutter of his
camera to capture the image of the newly wedded
couple before him: she circled the entire garden, majestically mounted the staircase leading to the terrace:
the train of your gown sweeping along behind you:
the nuptial bed was waiting
my gown?
encolure en pointe largement échancrée, taille haute,
garniture de tuyautés, jupe à panneau droit devant et
ampleur plongeante dans le dos, manches volantées,
coiffe, bouquet de petites anémones
a sudden tug, a violent struggle, he tears it off you
venez voir ce que lit la mémé!: un prospectus de
Pronuptia, la Maison du Bonheur: elle veut se marier
en blanc!

64

giggles, joking remarks, the others gathering round,
reading aloud captious questions, peals of laughter
do as I do: don't listen to them: they refuse to accept
the evidence, they persist in denying you
let's go back to the room, to our simple love nest, to
the modest fanduq in Marrakech
a cheap hotel next to the bus station, bootblacks,
travelers, pimps, errand boys, mountebanks, hustlers:
I stroll about, you stroll about in the tolerant atmosphere of the public square, courted, sought after,
overwhelmed by the clever complicity of images,
voices, groping hands, oneiric visions: a heraldic feu-
dal lady enveloped in the loving affection of her vassals: flattery, flowers, flirtatious remarks, intimate
whispers, courtly courtesies
I was still a virgin, my love: only recently recovered
from the sublime marvelous operation: discreetly
seeking someone to whom to offer her cavity, her
receptacle, her hollow: my miraculous grotto of
Lourdes
the magic ring of spectators hints at the recondite
presence so eagerly stalked: a svelte burnished body
ready for the feast, poised to attack: young boys,
epheboi, adolescent transvestites overawed by your
imperious eloquence, your elegant, splendid, magnificent bearing
here it is: have a look

studio poses, amateur snapshots, old, dog-eared, faded photomat images: a rigid, sober-faced farm-hand dressed in his very best, with his arm resting on the base of a garish urn full of flowers: soldiers in jauntily tilted berets, one hand casually thrust in a pocket: long robes, high-buttoned tunics, djellabahs, turbans, mustaches, Moorish caps

shuffling through anonymous faces, arbitrarily assigning them names: how where when place circumstances day

observed closely all of a sudden by the drone standing outside her cell, eager perhaps to test your knowledge, skill, dexterity, expertise born of long years of professional experience

tu viens, mon gars?

no, that one doesn't come in either, he walks on, enters the next cell, prefers the clumsiness of a novice waiting, still patiently waiting closing time: the end of her shift, putting away her equipment, gathering her belongings together, going up the stairs, crossing the vestibule, stepping out into the street

not into the symmetrical streams of pedestrians docilely obeying the magical dictates of synchronized traffic lights, the whistles and jerky puppet-gestures of policemen, the insistent hum of the métro overhead, the cetacean bulk of buses, loneliness encapsulated in the gleaming bodies of private passenger cars,

aggressiveness, compartmentalization, isolation, free-floating anxiety
deserted thoroughfares, yellow caution lights blinking steadily, wandering shades, loners, emigrés, drunks, fleeting silhouettes
little girl, old hag, adult woman: it doesn't matter
herself at last

DAR DEBBAGH

why me, him, and not the others, them?: imperturbably leaning on the battlemented parapet of the esplanade with their binoculars, polaroids, glasses, kodaks, movie cameras, a tame, motley flock paying close attention to the polyglot commentaries of the impeccable official guide: a stereotypic dragoman in a white djellabah and an inverted red flowerpot, possessed of a number and a badge that properly identify him and invest him with learned, benign authority: a patronizing attitude underlined by the condescending gesture with which he points to the perverse souls in that lucrative hell in which you are rotting away: to that lasciate ogni speranza, voi ch'entrate that tacitly, gloomily presides over your foreordained fate: voici le quartier des tanneurs, Messieurs-dames, the picturesque old tannery: as the docile members of the flock observe, peer, lie in wait on the top of the wall, fleetingly appear at the cannon embrasures, riddle the condemned men with their weapons, aim threatening telephoto and zoom lenses at the creatures in the tanning pits: heat, an overpowering stench, clavicles sticking out, skinny rib cages, gnarled arms, nothing but skin and bones: for you, for me, the damned, the object of neutral curiosity or indulgent disdain immortalized in the images of a souvenir album, smiling, puffed up with pride, self-assured, naal d-din ummhum, I shit on their dead: and once again the why, why, O Lord, always them and never me, shame, humiliation, digust, and they call this living: questions, questions, in the stinking, stifling circular prison, nothing foredoomed me to this death, I was born light and free as a bird, I've dreamed of eden ever since I was a youngster, you measured the vastness of desert expanses, roamed wherever you pleased amid the dunes: the nomad's way of life, tending flocks, wandering freely, listening to folktales in the heat of the tent, the origin and epitome of your rudimentary sensibility: plans, fantasies, illusions to which one clings desperately, like a shipwreck victim to his life preserver: a necessary compensation in the face of a harsh, cruel reality: working slouched over, bent almost double in the stinking hole, plucking off the bits of fleece stuck to the animal's skin, dressing the hide, laying the skins out flat in the sun, enduring the brutal mistreatment, the stench, the flies, trying to escape: getting out of there, fleeing with your suffering fellows, swearing never to come back, walking like a robot through the great free and alien city, heading toward the graceful silhouette of the Kutubia, stretching your hands out, palms joined, toward the minaret, invoking the justice of Allah, beseeching him to receive you in his kingdom, taking refuge in the higher certainty of eden, remembering the exact description of paradise: sweet repose, a cool place to sleep during the heat of the day, a garden full of trees and vines, shady bowers, exquisite silks, rivers of honey, abundant fruit: effacing the memory of your experience in the great city: digging like a mole, buried in a pit even darker and narrower than the pits of the tannery: recreating: gently flowing streams, incorruptible water, milk whose delicious taste never changes, maidens in the bloom of youth, nuptial pavilions, wine that does not intoxicate: going back nonetheless: scorching air, a

camel parched with thirst, a sere, barren plain: a life
sentence, wretched slavery, men swarming like lo-
custs, empty ears of grain with nothing left but bris-
tles: an orphan still, filthy, in tatters, the smell of
hides stubbornly clinging to my skin, bearing with
you the crushing burden of humiliation, downfall,
decrepitude, his miserable portable poverty: enveloped in the scorn and reproof of the elect, unwit-
tingly contaminating their air: go on, yes, go on,
don't stop, don't pay any attention, walk along like a
blind man, never let your eyes meet theirs: making
your way through the native quarter on foot, becoming inured to the fear of those who warily move away
as you draw near, retracing his footsteps in a delirious
daze without stretching out my black beggar's hand
to believers or to infidels: paying, paying, forever paying, for a roof overhead, light, food, paying, paying,
that's what we were born into this world for!: the pit
again, standing knee-deep in mud, scrubbing skins,
dressing the hide, laying it out in the sun like a stiff
tortoise pounded flat: deaf to the noisy presence of
the onlookers watching from the bastion in the wall
up above: the puzzled, perplexed flock awaiting instructions and explanations from the guide: a package tour flown in on a jet, on a direct flight from the
industrial smog of Pennsylvania: oh dear, look down

there at those men, it's just unbelievable!: straw hats, dark glasses, their proboscises protected from the sun by little sheets of cigarette paper or unnerving plastic noseguards: bearing a vague resemblance to creatures from outer space or victims of an accident just out of the hospital: absorbed in rapt contemplation of the condemned men peopling that vivid illustration of Dante's minutely detailed, geometrical delirium: of his body bent nearly double, his back scorched by the sun, his skull wrapped in a ragged turban, his pants legs hunched up around his thighs: vainly attempting to hide from others' eyes the one and only luxurious gift that God has given you: a dusky, pulsating ace of clubs, the involuntary cause of their derision, envy, stupefaction: seemingly submissive, but in reality intractable, rebellious, pertinacious, ever ready to poke its head out below the lower edge of the cloth at the slightest provocation or moment of inattention on your part: your condemned fellows know this, and refer to it periphrastically each time that you inadvertently display it as you straighten up after bending over: a discreet homage to the dimensions of a weapon that had aroused jealousy and awe in the days, at once so recent and so long ago, of your brief, ephemeral youth: working, continuing to toil away, to struggle with the animal skins, standing up to your knees in the filthy water, resting your eyes by gazing at the insubstantial shadow of the mosque, dimly aware of the guide's explanations and running commentary for the benefit of the tourists standing far overhead on the wall: closing your eyes, escaping, fleeing, blotting out the inferno, the outside world, paying no attention to their cameras, ignoring these spectators as they are ignoring me, all they want is to enjoy the show, to take advantage of the view from that impregnable fortress, a way of killing time: walking through the city, turning your palms toward the Kutubia, searching for an explanation of the disasters that have overtaken you, repeating your questions: penury, orphanhood, a merciless sun, a motionless, arrested, empty present: calling up memories of your childhood sheltered from hunger and storms, when you ran freely about the pasturelands, your gaze capturing life itself, your mother assured you that you would be the best, the strongest, the most beloved: today he is shunned by one and all, I bear the stigmata of misfortune, his friends avoid him in terror: you are the walking leper, the monster, the carrier of the plague: fleeing the horror, joining the other condemned men, seeking refuge in the tannery: a naked, dull gray, lunar expanse riddled with little round pits, like the scars of a stubborn case of smallpox: one for each condemned man: down into the hole, splashing about in the mud, dressing hides, a living death: aware of extraterrestrial eyes staring at your bent back, your bony arms, your skinny legs: the useless weight of your inflexible tail bound to your thighs by your trousers: restlessness, excitement, tumult among the lady spectators from Pennsylvania: the blonde beauty, in an exquisite white dress, whispers to her neighbor, focuses her binoculars on him, appears to lose herself in profound thought: a fluffy hairdo set in waves, like the top of a vanilla ice cream cone: patriotic, presbyterian, antisegregationist, abrahamlincolnesque blue eyes: meticulously outlined red lips of a pinup girl or a fashion model: a living example of the basic civic virtues of the Pilgrims: abstemiousness, frugality, a firm belief in the merits of fair play, progress, individualism: doubtless the wife of an executive with polarized sunglasses and a plastic nose, directly transported by air from the offices of Koppers or US Steel: all at once finding herself standing on the edge of the pit in which you are struggling with the hides: pretty, polite, spotless, betraying not the slightest sign of repugnance: apparently deeply interested in the traditional method of tanning skins and its breathtaking, fascinating exoticism: or perhaps in the sudden, scandalous proportions that your bare, absolutely functional tool has assumed: as cunning and crafty as a fractious, mischievous child; suavely releasing it from the pressure of the cloth and giving it its freedom, a proud and noble warrior: courteously offering his hand to the woman, helping her down to the sumptuous bed of the tanning pit: plunging her in the mud up to her knees, clasping her tightly in your eager, filthy arms, pressing my violent body to hers, sullying her pure white garments, voraciously kissing her red lips: still paralyzed with shocked surprise when with clumsy hands you pull up her skirts, paw her delicate pubis, her smooth convergent thighs, her silky black triangle: rubbing her vulva, introducing your sticky fingers in her vagina, lubricating, readying, preparing the way for the contained fury of your instrument: taking your pleasure, wallowing with her in the dirty water, kneading her breasts, straddling her hips, coupling within full view of the horrified tourists in the mirador, paying no attention to their exclamations and outcries, effacing your previous differences in pigmentation with slime and unbridled lust: the two of you burning, burning with passion as the ex-blonde creature laughs and hurls insults at the cuckolded executive, leaning his elbows on the edge of the tower, peering through his binoculars: iwa, el khal ka idrabni, yak?

ila bghiti tchuf ahsen ma-itjaf-ch, axi ḥdana!: no, that's not how it is, she stays up there with him, with the others, blonde, inaccessible, perfect, at the top of the crenelated wall: heat misery flies for me, everything for them, I fooled myself, they fooled me, I was born free and happy, I watched over the flocks, the shade of the trees was a promise and a symbol of the cool shade that awaited me in eden, young girls and boys followed me, we made love to each other in the dunes: like fire, yes, like fire, faces, garments, smiles, sprinkle the whole thing with gasoline, cigarette lighter, matches, whatever, my eyes flamethrowers, destruction, trails of phosphorus, screams, human torches: the pits again, animal skins, the dead desolation of the tannery, beauty close at hand and unattainable: without a voice, my tongue useless to me, no one willing to listen to what he has to say: they have ears and do not hear, they look at me and do not see me, my presence is an illusion, you are transparent, they are contemplating a specter: dressing hides, scraping off the fleece, putting up with the stench, abandoned to his fate, just a few yards away from the mosque: your long appendage hangs down like a dead weight, love eludes you, as empty as a mirage: useless to say ya baad-lah ghituní: they are immunized, and continue on their way, keeping their distance: a powerful spell binds him to the tannery,

forces him to return to the pit day after day, to
wander through the native quarter like a sleepwalker:
the freedom of the public square, its open spaces,
seem forbidden and inaccessible to me: dreaming,
continually dreaming of them, of losing his inability
to speak, of recovering my voice, of addressing the
crowds that flock about the entertainers in the halca:
pouring out a rush of words for hours on end: vomiting up dreams, tales, stories till you've emptied yourself out: and then waking up again, succumbing to
the curse, returning to the pit, getting stuck in the
mud: walking along with my flaccid pendulum dangling inertly, a shadow of myself, my youth and vigor
suppressed, barren, apathetic, a craven coward
watch the freak, it would be perfect for the sketch,
you could show him on the stage!
a pair of bearded men are watching him, run after
him, catch up with you, try to strike up a conversa-
tion with me
vu parlé fransé?
no, you don't understand them, what do they want
from me, they're talking European, a crowd gathers
round us, they insist that you go with them
venir avec nu, you understand? nu aller vu payer:
tien, here's some flus for you!
taking off with them like a whirlwind, public gardens, long straight avenues, buses, horse-drawn

carriages, clanging bells, squealing brakes, human
rivers, the Kutubia, Foucauld Square, the Club Médi-
terranée, ocher taxis, traffic cops, hustle and bustle,
exhibitions, speeches, dances, gymnastic feats
bold jaunty young
the evil spell miraculously broken
they take him away, you are, I am in the irregular
polygon of the main square

LE SALON DU MARIAGE

from the bus stops, the specially reserved parking lot, the exits of the closest subway station, the visitors hurry along toward the fabulous exhibition in compact groups: nuclear families, easily identifiable by their cohesion and the common denominator of a stereotypic smile: papa-mama-offspring-granny, who have come just to have a look around, to relive moments of joy, dim memories of bliss: future protagonists as well, with their panoply of illusions intact: eager to reach the oasis of voluptuous felicity, the wondrous, longed-for island: tenderly holding hands, as though they they were already joined forevermore: breaking into a run from time to time, with him in the lead and her in tow behind, both of them brimming over with good health and optimism, spontaneity, the attractiveness of youth: vite, dépêche-toi, regarde la queue, peut-être qu'ils vont fermer le guichet avant qu'on y arrive!: following their example, stepping up your pace, trying your best to keep your balance in your spike-heeled shoes: striding resolutely down the street, behind the crowd mesmerized by the mellifluous music pouring forth from the loudspeaker: docilely obeying the magnetic force generated by the sublime event: the apotheosis of century upon century of mating: happiness, good luck, prosperity within reach of every purse: crossing the boulevard when the traffic lights change: running into the roadblock of a prize-winning family in a national birth rate contest: breaking the chain of hands at the weakest link: rudely separating the little girl dressed like a page from her vernal little prince: assuming an air of offended dignity as you walk past the parents: at the end of the huge serpent patiently slithering toward the ticket window: not daring to talk about you, but you know that they are staring at you: puzzled by the inscrutable riddle of your identity: afraid that the children will suddenly give voice to the question that is inwardly tormenting them:

80

employing the flimsiest of pretexts in a vain attempt to distract their attention: victims of their rigid, antiquated principles of urbanity: exaggerating my regal impatience, lavishing extravagant gestures upon the crowd and making outlandish faces, compounding the general confusion: asking the couple standing next to me, for instance, in a cultivated foreign acent: excusez-moi, quel est le prix de l'entrée pour les jeunes filles? and greeting their response, je ne sais pas, mais je crois que c'est dix francs pour tout le monde sauf les moins de sept ans with an ah, bon, alors il n'y a pas de demi-tarif pour moi? accompanied by an insolent, childish pout of annoyance: reading their thoughts, divining their furtive smiles as we gradually move closer to the entrance: we arrive at the box office, you buy yourself a ticket, I hop onto the escalator: ascending slowly and gently, as in a dream, to the earthly paradise: a Shiraz carpet strewn with flower petals, cascades of draperies, red and saffron-yellow velvet, attractive little alcoves that smell of perfume and incense: clouds of mousseline de soie constitute the background of an exquisite tableau of palm trees and ferns artistically sprinkled with dewdrops: a profusion of mirrors multiply the countenances of damsels with headdresses and veils of gleaming white satin: arriving at the frontier of eden, the slight, symbolic customs barrier: little low tables

covered with brochures and file cards, hostesses in
impeccable uniforms, an atmosphere of gracious,
honeyed hospitality: ritual questions asked with a
pleasant, immutable smile: voici notre carte et docu-
mentation, c'est vous les futurs mariés? la cérémonie
est prévue pour quand?: mechanically smoothing
your dress as you await your turn, glancing in the
dizzying succession of mirrors to make certain every
hair is in place: giving the quietus to possible scornful remarks with haughty gestures, planting myself
squarely in front of the first free hostess and savoring
the sudden cruel shock of the impact: the hair, the
tunic, the two days' growth of beard: aware of the
interest that your presence is arousing, of the fact that
I am, as always, the cynosure of all eyes: insidiously
waiting a few sconds for the hostess to begin the
dialogue
voici la fiche d'inscription, c'est pour vous?
oui, mademoiselle
voulez-vous que je vous la remplisse?
oui, s'il vous plaît
votre nom?
je vais vous l'épeler, car c'est difficile: ele-a-ef-o-dou-
ble ele-a: comme la folle, mais avec une *a* à la fin
prénom?
je n'ai pas de prénom, chez nous ça n'existe pas, vous

savez?: on a un nom, et c'est tout!: c'est beaucoup
plus pratique!
glancing all about you as if to garner people's looks of
approval and proudly assure yourself that they are
listening to you
et votre fiancée?
mon fiancé, mademoiselle
oh, votre fiancé!
Ahmed, il s'appelle Ahmed, il est militaire, voici sa
photo
rummaging about in your handbag, fishing out a
faded snapshot, handing it to the hostess with a
youthful, impulsive gesture, silently enjoying her
foreseeable reactions of surprise and hesitation
il est beau, n'est-ce pas?
the hostess, curtly:
oui, très beau: enfin, voilà la fiche: vous pouvez la
compléter vous-même et nous l'envoyer par la poste
sans besoin de l'affranchir
merci beaucoup, mademoiselle: et ça?
c'est le Guide des Futurs Époux
je peux en prendre un?
allez-y, il est à vous
oh, comme vous êtes charmante!
taking the colored pamphlet, on the cover of which is
a drawing, in pink, of that hollow, muscular thoracic

83

vital part, shaped like a cone, which is the principal organ responsible for the circulation of the blood, and inside it a bride and groom heading toward a castle decorated in turn with a flag bearing two equally pink but minuscule hearts: opening the Guide at random and leafing through the calendar countdown intended to refresh the memory of the future contracting parties.

Rencontre entre les deux familles pour fixer la date et mettre au point tous les détails matériels concernant le mariage et l'installation du jeune ménage

Pour une cérémonie religieuse, aller à l'église pour s'enquérir de toutes les pièces à produire et des démarches à faire

Établir votre "liste de mariage"

Choisir les témoins, demoiselles d'honneur et les pages, s'assurer de leur accord, prévoir leur tenue

going down the first aisle of the exhibition, stopping in front of the snow-white, psychedelic Pronuptia stand: dozens of mannequins frozen in lithe, graceful postures: a symphony of colors in mauve, lilac, violet tones, coordinated bridesmaids' gowns in a delightfully old-fashioned, romantic silk print: ostrich plumes tinted to match rose, fuchsia, daffodil dresses in mousseline de soie: Calais lace, embroidered tulle veils, flowered bridal wreaths, an exquisite parasol: absorbing, enraptured, the hostess's running commentary on the ballet of flesh-and-blood models, immortalized in the supreme perfection of their attire: for their wedding day, Virginie and Patrick have decided to be young and gay: she has chosen a very poetic gown in a delicate flower print, with an anti-traditional low-cut neckline and an ample skirt with a ruffled train: he, an advocate of casual dress, has selected a white duck suit with a discreet pin-stripe: you will agree that the couple is a model of beauty, self-assurance, suppleness

noting the admiring remarks being exchanged by your neighbors: oh, comme c'est, joli, il te faudrait un complet comme ça, au fond ce n'est pas cher, ils font du crédit, tu sais? on peut toujours le payer à tempérament!: asking the icy hostess for a price list: from the Icarus number, in polyester crêpe de Chine, to the Etincelle, with a veil and an embroidered headband: stroking the tulle headdress of Nuée and asking in a falsetto voice if it would look good on you: isn't there a try-on room somewhere in the place?: no, there isn't one, this is only an exhibition, if this model interests you we'll give you the number of it and arrange for you to try it on at our branch store that's handiest for you: there's no hurry, miss, I'll come back tomorrow, after I've been to the barbershop!

murmurs of disapproval, comments in a furtive whisper, stifled giggles: it's unbelievable, what nerve, coming here to make fun of decent folk, no respect even for families, there's nothing some people won't do these days!: turning a deaf ear, taking refuge in a heavy silence: contemplating your face in the mirror, smoothing your eyebrows, stroking the stubble on my chin: saying with an annoyed expression to your neighbor: ça pousse si vite! comment faites-vous pour vous épiler le visage? burying yourself, without waiting for her to reply, in your reading of the countdown Guide

Retenir la salle dans l'établissement où sera fait le lunch ou le repas du mariage

Commander le faire-part à l'imprimeur

Réserver définitivement le logement et prévoir l'équipement nécessaire: mobilier, cuisine, électroménager, literie, textiles d'ameublement, etc. Faire établir un devis aux fournisseurs. N'hésitez pas à examiner le plus grand nombre possible de propositions. Souvenez-vous: le dernier mot vous appartient!

going on to the next stand, getting lost in a maelstrom of advice, handy hints, offers: turn everyday living into something marvelous!: in the magazine A Hundred Ideas you'll find each month a hundred pages or more of dreams and instructions on how to

make them come true, useful tips on knitting, cro-
cheting, embroidering, sewing, cooking, giving free
rein to your inventiveness and creativity!: a hundred
ideas, from the most practical to the most unusual,
the ultimate in sophistication!: another pamphlet: to
decorate your home from cellar to attic and turn it
into a Dream Palace: a giant close-up of a wilted rose:
don't waste your money on something that doesn't
last: our flowers are choicer than ever this year: they
imitate nature to perfection and have the precious
advantage of remaining fresh forever
reading, gathering information, cherishing fond
hopes, entertaining tempting illusions, losing yourself in fascinated contemplation of the wondrous list
of reminders in the Guide
Préparer le voyage de noces et faire les réservations
Vérifier passeports et vaccinations s'il y a lieu
Choisir les alliances afin de pouvoir les faire graver
*Votre armoire de linge de maison est-elle suffisamment
garnie?*
*Avez-vous le nécessaire en linge de lit, linge de table, linge
de toilette, linge de cuisine?*
following a zigzag path as you continue your anxious
search, joining a vast group of bystanders and listening to the hypnotic suggestions of the uniformed
sibyl on duty at the stand: give the computer the

place, date, and hour of your birth and that of your intended and in ten days' time you will receive a specially prepared text, based on both your horoscopes, that will tell you, with the minimum margin of error possible, what ups and downs you will face in your love life: Astroflash analyzes what unites and separates married couples: thanks to your prior knowledge of potential obstacles, you will find yourself better prepared to overcome them and thereby ensure that your future will be a radiantly happy and prosperous one!

approaching the snow-white, immaculate angel of the annunciation and timidly putting the problem before her: will it be enough if you have the necessary data on just one of us?: mon fiancé ne connaît pas l'année de sa naissance: confronting without blinking an eye her freezingly polite smile: his parents doubtless remember: a contrite expression: he's an orphan, miss: doesn't he have a certificate of baptism from the parish priest?: he's never been baptized, I say, il est africain: well then, she says, all he needs to do is go to the city hall and apply for a copy of his birth certificate: but he doesn't know which city hall either, you say: he was born in the desert, do you follow me?: puzzlement on the part of the boreal hostess, brazen curiosity on the part of the bystanders: well, in that case, what can I tell you?: turning to the onlookers, taking them as witness: mon Dieu, quel pari, s'unir pour toujours à un homme bleu sans savoir si nos astres sont vraiment compatibles!: appealing to a rosy-cheeked girl who is staring at me in open-mouthed stupefaction: what would you do if you were in my shoes, miss?: would you follow your fiancé to the end of nowhere, to the tiny garrison lost amid the sand dunes where he's stationed?: silence, astonishment, stifled titters: general suspense as one and all await her answer

saying not a word, leaving them the pleasure of exchanging reproving and mocking remarks about you once you have gone, proudly walking away, girded in lofty disdain as though promoted to a more exalted rank

Et pourquoi ne pas construire votre pavillon immédiatement? Parce que vous n'avez pas assez d'argent, dites-vous? N'êtes-vous pas mal informés? Des facilités que vous n'aurez plus après, sont accordées uniquement dans les deux ans de votre mariage

Être chez soi pour le prix d'un loyer, c'est possible!

S'assurer du financement indispensable, faire la demande de crédit nécessaire. Le prêt d'Etat de 6.000 F remboursable en 48 mensualités égales de 125 F sans intérêt, peut être sollicité dès la publication des bans

interrupting your reading of the Guide: another stand, another hostess, another sales pitch: slipping into the semicircle of onlookers, sharing their devout, well-nigh mystical, attentiveness, allowing myself to be caressed, like a pampered cat, by the grave, sedative murmur of her voice

queen of genuine precious stones, the diamond is the most beautiful token of love and fidelity that man has known since time immemorial: the very symbol of imperishable sentiment, from the early days of antiquity there has been attributed to it a magic power that aids and protects those who wear it: encased in a magnificent box, this noble and prestigious ring is sold with a numbered certificate attesting to its authenticity: hand-cut, a written warranty, an unbelievable price, an absolutely safe investment!

elbowing your way through the crowd, inspecting the various models, comparing prices, slipping the flashiest ring onto the third finger of your left hand beneath the reproving gaze of your neighbors, admiring its sparkling reflections on your bony outstretched hand

our days are numbered: prudence counsels you to place your order without delay: don't miss out on this opportunity: this is a limited offer!

mademoiselle?: combien fait cette bague?

2850 francs, mais vous profitez pendant toute la se-
maine d'un 20% de réduction
she turns around: she looks at me: her smile suddenly
disappears
elle est bien trop large pour vous!
elle n'est pas pour moi, mademoiselle: je cherche une
alliance pour mon fiancé
ah, bon
pause: the time necessary for her to recover from her
astonishment, to regain her self-control
connaissez-vous ses mesures?
modesty, a deliberately chaste expression, a sudden
virginal blush suffusing your cheeks
elles sont inoubliables, mademoiselle!
but she doesn't understand, or pretends not to understand: impassivity, stern self-control, the merest hint
of a frown: she watches you closely as you remove the
ring from your finger: instinctively polishing it with
a cloth when you hand it back, as though you'd dirt-
ied it: returning it to its splendid case
a child's voice behind me: tu as vu, papa? la dame n'a
pas rasé sa barbe!: a predictable slap, followed by
weeping: tais-toi, morveux!: the timely intervention
of the hostess: going on with her sales pitch
a famous artist has created this double ring for you:
the fabulous model called Inseparable: two strands of

91

gold forever entwined like two hearts united for life!:
our 24-carat gold-plated rose is also most unusual:
gathered in the gardens of Versailles, this flower will
be preserved forever in all its admirable beauty: fashioned by a goldsmith of genius, it is the best possible
gift you can offer the one you love as proof of a
sentiment as enduring as the rose itself!: various sizes
at prices that will leave you breathless! reliability and
dependability are the cornerstones of our philosopy!
paying no heed to the hostility that envelops me:
confronting ignominy like a monarch recently de-
throned: with the serenity of an Austro-Hungarian
duchess contemplating her castle burning to the
ground

*Préparer la liste de mariage. Ce n'est pas de mauvais usage,
tout au contraire, de la répartir dans plusieurs magasins
spécialisés*

*Demander au commerce de cadeaux où la liste a été envoyée
de prévenir parents et amis éloignés que vous n'avez encore
pas eu l'occasion d'informer personnellement. Nous serons
heureux de déposer dans votre corbeille de Mariés votre
premier cadeau: une réduction "nouveaux mariés" de
50%!*

there's a weirdo for you if there ever was one! absolutely shameless! what's an oddball like that doing
here anyway?: what's more, that outlandish creature

seems to be laughing at us! what the devil's going on:
I've never seen such cheek in all my born days!
abruptly wheeling about, finding yourself face to face
with a reserved young lady and her fiancé disguised as
an executive: giving her a sly, knowing smile: opening your purse: taking out a package of cigarettes
would you give me a light please?
I'm sorry, I don't smoke
you're quite right not to, dearie: I should be like you
and not smoke either: they say that it's deadly dangerous when you're pregnant: but I'm all nerves at
the moment: my fiancé's arriving tomorrow!
another stand: to allow your wedding guests to share
your happiness and offer them an original souvenir of
the ceremony to keep forever, we advise you to give
each of them his or her very own wedding gift: a
darling box of matches with the date and your two
names engraved in gold
if you don't have money, invest! in the romantic
dawn of your life together, you are doubtless dreaming of a beautiful, roomy apartment of your very
own, a spacious dwelling destined to ensure your future family's privacy: but such a thing seems impossible for the moment: you unfortunately do not have
sufficient savings put aside: we offer you the solution
to your problem: invest immediately in our agency:

with our help you will one day have the capital necessary to purchase the marvelous home you dream of!
mademoiselle: you will soon be united for life to the
man you love: for his sake, for your own sake, be the
fairest one of all!: make your wedding a poem, dress
your happiness in white!: admire the photographs in
our catalogue and read it attentively: the bridal
gown, your wedding dress, the one you dream of at
night, the one you've yearned for ever since you were
a little girl, has been created especially for you by our
fashion designers!

looking out of the corner of your eye at those who are
staring at you: groups from the provinces, the big
family encountered outside on the street, Japanese
tourists with their Japanese movie cameras: continuing to nose about the place: male models, with perfectly posed hips and kneecaps, impeccable tuxedos, a
candid smile, a virile, protective gaze: cocktail parties,
banquets, wedding suppers, equipment for recep-
tions, chefs, butlers, waiters, hostesses, atmosphere,
shows, spectacles, sound effects: twenty-five years'
experience, branches in all provinces!: consulting
pamphlets, making calculations, voicing opinions,
seeking inspiration in the Guide

*Choisir le menu et demander confirmation des prix au
traiteur*

Chercher un photographe, assurer le reportage de la céré-

monie au magnétoscope, organiser votre réception et votre
voyage de noces
Prendre rendez-vous chez le notaire pour le consulter sur le
Régime Matrimonial
reaching the end of the exhibition hall, turning to
the right, starting down another aisle: retouching
your makeup with the aid of a little mirror: asking a
hostess where the ladies' room is: gleefully noting her
indignant expression
in the back to the right!
thank you, mademoiselle: do you know if the atten-
dant has sanitary napkins?
stupefaction, contained fury, she abruptly turns her
back to me: greeting with a serene gaze the looks of
consternation on the faces of your neighbors: hum-
ming a song by Dalida: raising the pitch of your voice
ex professo
come on, Martine, let's go, this is scandalous!
this isn't a transvestite show, do you hear?
no, you don't, you pretend not to understand, I flash
him a smile: girls wearing dresses shown in *Elle* and
Marie Claire: radiant couples, affable couples, bored
couples, elegant couples, couples about to couple
the train is about to pull out: the leavetaking is a
joyous one: who can doubt that the newlyweds are
headed straight for happiness? the bridesmaid is wearing an ecru lace gown: the flower girl looks adorable

95

in her organdy dress with a red satin sash: the little page boy is as cute as a button in his green velvet pants and white middy blouse: the mother of the bride has chosen a dress in filmy mousseline de soie and a delicate shawl: they have all had the marvelous idea of outfitting themselves for the wedding in our stores!

another stand: the Personal Library of the Future Couple

Five Thousand Recipes

The Ideal Home

Man and Woman

Sexual Harmony

Legal Handbook of Marriage Laws

to make your guests laugh and ensure that your party will be a lively affair: comic monologues, risqué songs, a repertory of bawdy jokes, decks of cards that hint at the joys of the wedding night: our extraordinary catalogue of trick gadgets: sneezing powder, collapsing knives, surprise sugar lumps: when they melt in your guests' coffee, they will discover a fly, a tooth, a cockroach, and so on in the bottom of their cups!

party favors shaped like hand grenades, hidden underneath paper napkins: when the wick is lighted there's a terrific explosion and your guests will receive a fantastic shower of gifts: indispensable for creating a festive atmosphere!

glasses that look like ordinary ones but are impossible to drink from: a good joke on the frustrated drinker, great fun for all those present!

shoot a stream of ink all over your neighbor's shirt: he won't know that the stain is removable and will have the shock of his life!

a gimmick hidden in your pocket that produces a cow's moo: this perfect imitation of a prolonged bellow will amaze your friends!

a flower that squirts water: invite your pals to smell it and squeeze the bulb: bound to be a success!

stationmaster's whistles to send the bride and groom on their way: an original way of starting them off on their honeymoon and wishing them the very best of luck!

a crowd of curious bystanders gathering: but they're not looking at the stand: they're eyeing me: a girl with rosy apple-cheeks: a fiancé dressed like a store-window dummy: dull couples, colorless couples: impassioned antimalthusian families

taking a cigarette out of your purse, inserting it in an amber holder, asking a middle-aged man for a light, thanking him effusively, exhaling a mouthful of smoke with exquisite pleasure

going up to the counter of a real estate agency specializing in private homes: villas, country houses, town houses: the most important purchase you will

ever make!: examining the price list, scale models of
the various types of dwellings available, the guaran-
tees and credit terms: politely asking the sales representative if they have jaimas
he: nastily
qu'est-ce que c'est?
une sorte de tente, mais beaucoup plus large
pour faire du camping?
non, pour y vivre dedans, I say: comme celles des
cheiks dans le désert: vous avez vu le film de Va-
lentino?
no, he hasn't seen it
c'est dommage! le décor est charmant!
he: aggressively
vous êtes venu ici pour me parler de cinéma?
not at all, you say: je cherche une orientation
he: rudely
allez vous faire orienter ailleurs!: on n'a rien à foutre
avec des gens de votre acabit!
what to do? forgive him? play the prima donna?: take
out a calling card and announce to him that you're
sending round your seconds for a duel?: give him a
resounding slap in the face?: the onlookers are taking
in the whole scene with obvious glee: the credibility
of the role I'm playing is at stake: you must maintain
it at all costs

je dirai à mon fiancé combien vous êtes insolent!:
vous aurez bientôt de ses nouvelles!

voices, murmurs, exclamations: you turn your back
on your adversary with an air of great dignity, majestically continuing on down the aisle: kitchens, dining rooms, studies: twin beds, innerspring mattresses,
studio couches, countless double beds: thanks to its
original structure, the Multicoil mattress ensures you
a restful night's sleep, guaranteed to restore your
nerves and your physical energy: perfect suspension:
air-conditioned models: contributes to the happiness
of your marriage: consult our specialists today!

receiving, advising, guiding couples is not only our
motto: for us it is also a legitimate source of pride!

whether you are planning a wedding celebration
strictly limited to members of your families or a feast
for hundreds or even thousands of guests, don't resort to a disastrous improvisation that you will regret
all the rest of your life: let our technicians organize it
for you: your success depends entirely on you: just
pick up your telephone!

dishes, glassware, porcelain, damask tablecloths will
add their luster to the elegance and variety of the food
served: floral decorations, polychromed sculptures of
fruits and other viands will contribute to creating the
refined atmosphere that you and your fiancé desire: a

reception is composed like a symphony: a party, like a classic altarpiece: music, lighting, décor will cast their magic spell in delightful harmony with our catered dishes and our wines: the art of entertaining is our business: contact us!

with each step my presence attracts the curiosity of bystanders like a magnet

hey, did you get a look at that?: wow, a real ass-slinger!: don't laugh, I don't think it's a bit funny!: if it were up to me, I'd shoot the whole lot of them! ah, come off it, will you, it's best simply to ignore them!

feigning self-absorption, indifference till you arrive at a stand full of angels, hearts, doves, plunged in an intimate, comfortable half-shadow

> Songe qu'avant d'unir nos
> têtes vagabondes, nous avons
> vécu seuls, séparés, égarés,
> et que c'est long, le temps
> et que c'est grand, le monde
> et que nous aurions pu ne pas
> nous rencontrer

you are carried away by the charm, the tenderness, the profundity of this poetic sentiment: you need to communicate your emotions, share them with your neighbors, as a person might share with others a rare and exquisite dish

c'est vrai, ça!: mon fiancé vit loin, très loin, en Afrique!: si je n'avais pas fait une tournée artistique dans les casernes des méharistes nous ne nous serions jamais connus!: vous vous rendez compte de la chance merveilleuse qu'on a eu?

a fixed and inscrutable expression on the woman's face: a scornful gesture on the part of her spouse: for the space of an instant he seems to be on the point of answering you, but she tugs insistently at his arm and the two of them walk away with an air of offended dignity

you deserve to be happy: don't just dream of having a home and a family!: resolve to do so

break out, once and for all, of the infernal circle of isolation: happiness is within your reach: getting married through our agency doesn't mean giving up the spirit of conquest, if you're a man, or the desire to be attractive, if you're a woman!

our century is the age of specialization: if we consult an attorney in order to find a solution to a difficult legal problem or visit a doctor in order to remedy our precarious state of health, why rely solely on our own resources when it comes time to make the most serious and important decision of our entire lives?: why trust in chance alone when one has only a limited circle of friends and acquaintances within which it is impossible to realize to the fullest one's most secret aspirations?

once you have consulted us, we will set up a confidential file, based on the results of our interview of you and your answers to our questionnaire, in which anything and everything that might help us to know your personality, your very own self, will be meticulously noted: after a detailed study of your case, we will select, with extreme care, from our list of candidates whose desires roughly correspond to yours, the man or woman who turns out to share the most subtle affinities with you, physically, mentally, and emotionally: the fact that you know beforehand that such affinities exist will enhance your desire to know the person chosen better, to explore with him or her all the sources of his or her personal attraction: a meeting under such circumstances becomes an exciting adventure in the most noble sense of the word!
there is no one better than us at bringing a couple together, harmonizing two personalities, playing the role of the good fairy who introduces to each other two beings destined since the beginning of time to meet each other, to love each other!
madame, vous avez une minute?: je voudrais vous poser une question
she: distrustful
allez-y, je vous écoute
j'ai déjà choisi mon fiancé: je l'aime et il m'aime aussi: mais nous ne connaissons pas encore nos goûts, nos

affinités: je ne comprends même pas un mot de son dialecte!: alors je voudrais savoir s'il pourrait se mettre éventuellement en contact avec vous

she: curtly

we are at your service

what I mean to say is: the problem is that he can't come to Paris: he's a master sergeant in a regiment of native sharpshooters, do you see what I mean?: might you possibly have a representative in Rissani, in the Tafilelt?

where did you say?

Rissani, in the Tafilelt: a lovely oasis south of the Atlas, on the very edge of the desert

she: visibly annoyed

I've never heard of such a place in my life!

you: with a look of surprise

well, it's on the map! it even has a public phone booth!

she: cuttingly

I'm sorry, but there's absolutely nothing we can do for you

and that was that: turning on your heels, taking leave of those following you with an aloof wave of your hand, adopting the pose of a cardinal of the Curia in his twilight years, his health undermined by a long and incurable illness: smiling feebly, throwing kisses as though you were tossing pieces of candy to the

103

crowd: sprinkling holy water with an invisible as-
pergillum: moving away from the faithful amid
Louis XV commodes, Louis XVI tables, Empire
dining room suites, Isabella II period furniture: mon-
archic cachet, aristocratic dreams, faded nobility
lectures on family planning: ensure your domestic
felicity thanks to the purchase, in cash or on credit, of
a superb set of kitchen equipment: our aim: ending
your loneliness forever: statistics concerning the gifts
most appreciated by newlyweds: vacuum cleaner
(95%), washing machine (83%), color TV set (70%),
dishwasher (58%): read together what each of the
two of you feels: our selection of the Hundred Best
Poems: the intimate physiology of the woman: learn
all about the female body!: let us plan your honeymoon for you: we will draw up a personalized itinerary for you, based on your secret fantasies: the Gate of
Paradise, the Forgotten Islands, the perfume of the
tropics, the land of the plumed serpent!
the vestibule again
the symblic customs barrier, guides, hostesses, smiles,
groups, couples, the escalator, descending from the
marvelous dream, going down and down, confronting the astonished faces of those going up, the line
again, the ticket window, rejecting reality, fleeing the
public, the crush of people, the traffic, living the unforgettable scene in the film, Morocco, the gate in the

wall, the magnate who's waiting in his Rolls and looks at you with a heartbroken expression, but you choose to follow your soldier-lover, to pass up wealth and social status for his sake, to hitch yourself to the yoke of whores and camp followers trailing along in the wake of the Moorish infantrymen and soldiers of the Legion, throwing away your useless spike-heeled shoes, treading the delicate ripples of the sand dunes in your bare feet, walking, walking, losing yourself in the desert

WINTER LODGINGS

the Cretan labyrinth?: the structure designed by De-
dalus?: the possible residence of a fabulous Minotaur
redivivus?: an extremely complicated layout in any
event: a succession of galleries, corridors, courtyards,
audience chambers, colonnades with marble pillars:
Le Vau, Mansart, Le Nôtre artistically presented in a
Sound and Light show?: or a modern, substitute version of sumptuous greatgatsbian mansions such as
The Breakers or Rosecliff?: because of its cryptic, hidden nature, the archeologist brave enough to venture
into it would find it difficult to identify immediately:

a city buried by a terrific volcanic explosion?: inhabitants caught by surprise in their dwellings by an incandescent lava flow?: cautiously entering by way of the little opening: a simple aperture or trapdoor presumably guarded by a fearsome, surly cerberus: perhaps absent from his post in order to fulfill higher, more conspicuous duties: repeating with rigorous exactitude the routine motions: squatting down, sliding back the ingenious device that conceals the entrance, testing each rung of the metal ladder, descending till you touch bottom, peering warily about to make certain no one is looking, throwing the booty down at the foot of the little ladder, fitting the heavy trapdoor back over the circular cement shaft: safe and sound and last: sovereign of the kingdom of infinite night: melting into it, become one with this powerful Avernus: emerging from the sewer opposite the Porta Marina, heading across the pedestrian walkway, disdaining the obsequious guides, warding off their aggressive offers to share their rusty knowledge, proceeding down the Via dell'Abbondanza, become my own, personal cicerone: dusky bare feet, insensitive to the rigors of the season?: ragged, threadbare pants with improvised skylights at the knees?: a scarecrow's overcoat with collar raised to conceal a double absence?: the wise decision of the authorities to keep the city in darkness mercifully shelters you from the piercing gaze of others: the pipes of the municipal heating system protect him from the inclement elements: walking on and on, like a blind man, without the aid of a dog, a guide, a cane: happy to forget for a few hours the crepuscular civilization of the world of light: under cover, defended, invulnerable, in the propitious fetal blackness: making my way through the Elysian Fields that lead to my quarters without fear of the naked aggression of traffic on the streets: master of the broad walk flanked by vast mansions: listening to the murmur of the crystal-clear stream gently flowing along the thoroughfare: deserted temples, villas, palaces: walls decorated with mosaics, frescoes with a red and black background, erotic scenes painted in gesso, grandiose friezes depicting mythological subjects: crossing the intersections in front of the forum and the basilica, the Terme Stabiane, the House of Menander: rubbing with callused fingers signs probably bearing warnings or words of welcome: Vale, Salve, perhaps the Cave Canem of a mistrustful householder: continuing on my way, endeavoring not to set foot inadvertently on someone else's property: the entryway or atrium of some wealthy, magnanimous, night-wandering patrician: usually visible thanks to the lictors' fasces: a feeble, flickering light that nonetheless suffices to reveal the ritual celebration of a banquet within the vast dwelling: a family agape, a simple country meal shared with talkative bosom companions and friends: guests reclining on triclinia with an aromatic elixir in hand: bottles discreetly concealed in the paper sacks of the local liquor store, the skillfully bottled blond fermentation of barley and hops: as meanwhile, filling in for the servants who are inexplicably absent, the wealthy host displays his talents as a seasoned gastronome, carefully seeing to it that all the viands are perfectly prepared and served: a cheery scene that he frequently comes upon in the course of a pleasant, picturesque, delightfully warm, cozy, heated journey homeward: amid harmonious, decorative little waterfalls on either side and vaults dripping with beautiful stalactites overhead: feeling his way through the agreeable darkness, trying his best not to stumble over a slumbering landowner, as has sometimes happened: your tripping over him by accident having rudely aroused him from the delicious drowsiness of his libations: empty wine jars strewn all around his lectum, no doubt left lying there due to the carelessness of his famulus: mumbling otiose apologies and hearing understandable growls of annoyance as you walk away: tempestuous desiderata having to do with his perverse pleasure or your damnation: usually formulated in cutting tones: I shit on your whore of a mother, you fairy! or something of the sort, in the cultivated accent of the native of Latium: continuing intrepidly on your way, happy to be deciphering at your leisure the sounds and the signs of life of the Vesuvian city: the interminable dripping of waste products, the sudden overflow of sewer outlets, the steamy emanations of burning-hot heating pipes: an ideal temperature, perennial summer, favorable to the rapid propagation of agile and intelligent domestic species: instead of felines or canines whose care and feeding involve a regrettable loss of time and, worse still, energy, Muridae marvelously adapted to the climatic conditions of these environs: perfect specimens with elegant coats, sensitive snouts, sharp eyes, that run about with the svelte litheness of the meticulously painted greyhounds in the friezes of antiquity: the daily escort of my journey to the winter palace buried beneath the capital: awaiting the tasty tidbits that you are in the habit of giving them on retiring to the strict privacy of your domicile: recognizing, with pleasure and a sense of relief, the simple, cherished objects of your lodgings: the accumulated product of past foraging expeditions in the asphalt jungles of the upper level: junk, odds and ends, trash of no nutritive value whatsoever to your boisterous addicts: installing yourself among them, lulled by the gentle murmur of the stream peacefully flowing through the sewer: opening your treasure sack with a generous gesture and offering the first fruits to my personal rodent: a voracious, omnivorous mouse fond of the delicate flavor of human cartilage: possessed of salivary glands with intense anesthetic powers that enable him to accomplish his amazing deeds without the most interested party even noticing: nothing but a slight itching sensation as he awakens from his slumbers: an instinctive movement: raising his hands to his ears and discovering to his astonishment that both of them are missing: a gesture repeated endlessly, with almost Luciferian pride, in the face of the anonymous, fierce multitude on the sidewalks: a black sheep, a mangy cur, an inharmonious parasite: a discordant instrument in the execution of a score: a metaphor lost amid the algebraic signs of an equation: the inferno, their world, blotted out: forgetting the city, the streets, the crowds: not seeing them, not noticing their presence, deliberately offering them an icy transparency, invisibility: unhurriedly stroking your livestock: your superb collection of chinchillas with lustrous reddish fur: proceeding to give each of them their fair share of the booty and watching the activity of their incisors with lingering delight: settling down in the warm hospitality of the bed, surrounded by their solicitous attentions and flattery: allowing them to run freely over your body, to nose about as they please amid your members and extremities: feet, head, hands, a naturally prominent organ that is the involuntary cause of panic, envy, stupefaction: freeing it from the pressure of the cloth so that it can move about at will, a proud and valiant warrior: a dark, pulsating ace of spades, the object of the care and affection of your faithful, devoted protégés: paws applying furtive friction, snouts paying slight homage gradually stimulate the astonishing transformation: a massive, lathe-turned column, the ideal recipient of vassals' tributes and offerings: coveted by transvestites, fled in terror by damsels, condemned by reason of its scandalous dimensions to the solitude and anonymity of the catacombs: a place of worship and pilgrimage for your assiduous attendants: a saraband of greedy bear cubs round a hive full of honey: fondling, fawning, caresses lavished with tireless diligence by tiny, rough carpet-tongues: a sophisticated, typically Pompeian specialty: a gourmet's delicacy, teasingly exquisite, at the farthest possible remove from the venal proficiency of the harlots immortalized in the frescoes of the brothel: making the tingling of their saliva more powerful by a subtle inhalation of cannabis: the pungent aroma of the mountains on the other side of the Mare Nostrum, in Numidia, your distant, longed-for homeland: ecstatically breathing in a fragrant puff, promptly forgetting the trials and tribulations of the day: the object

112

of the worshipful celebration of the Muridae gathered round your tangible charisma: lulled by the quiet murmur of the waters, warmed by the radiations of an invisible system of heating ducts, savoring my small, inalienable share of happiness: freed from the horror, loneliness, emptiness, the acute feeling of death that overcame him up above: like fire, yes, like fire, faces, garments, smiles, sprinkle the whole thing with gasoline, cigarette lighter, matches, whatever, my eyes flamethrowers, destruction, trails of phosphorus, screams, human torches: joyful images of retaliation, extra-sweet dreams of revenge, enhanced by the aroma of the cannabis and the syncopated strokings of your followers' little flicking lingual tails: epithelial vibration, a rush of blood, rigid tumefaction: the sudden acceleration of your pulsations presages an imminent volcanic eruption and heightens the ardor of the meticulous linguists: instead of a fervid, fatal emission of lava, a warm, thick, rich substance similar to that which bees distill from flowers and then deposit in the little cells of combs: licked up to the last drop by the impatient, obliging rodents, with characteristic promptness and deftness: sparing me the ancestral gesture of soaking it up with the folds of his patrician garment and rubbing the still-erect but now flaccid propulsive organ with dust or sand in obedience to the precepts regarding hygiene

113

laid down in the sacred Book: Coal Black and the Seven Ratamites, as well as in the polychrome prints of the film projected in the immense movie theater on the boulevard: rising from your bed of delights, passing out food and drink with a lavish hand, collecting water in the nearby impluvium and putting it on top of the burning-hot ducts of the calidarium to boil in a Campbell's soup can: a frugal repast, but abundant enough to restore his strength after my exhausting periplus about the enemy camp: the scrupulous repetition of the ceremony of imparting the remains of the agape to the merry minuscule flock, lying down on the soft expanse of the triclinium, enveloping feet and hands in multiple sheets of papyrus so as to prevent nocturnal feasting on the part of your domesticated rodents: lighting one last roll of hemp leaves, levitating through the friendly darkness in a caliginous state of bliss: wandering, hospitality, the nomad's way of life, vast expanses, other times, his language, my dialect, as in days long past, in their midst I live and move and have my being, free at last, heading toward the market

ANDROLATRESS

impossible to forget, to forget you
she searched for him, you searched for him in the
semidarkness of movie theaters, subway stations, little neighborhood cafés, more and more frantically,
without ever losing hope of catching up with you,
she was certain she'd run into you somewhere, she
thought constantly of the bliss of our first meeting,
your fierce criminal's face, the nocturnal splendor of
your private parts, until she happened, you happened
to hear about your tour, your celebrated exhibition in

circuses, the amazement of the spectators, and I put money aside, hoarded pennies like an ant in order to come here, a cloistered nun, devoted to your worship alone, shunning the world, meditation, chastity, vanity of vanities

occupations to kill time: removing excess hair, applying makeup, astrology, reading *Rêves, Intimité, Détective, Ici Paris, France Dimanche:* devoutly practicing androlatry: commiserating, sympathizing, identifying with its victims: Soraya, Margaret, Jacqueline, the bewitched blonde princess: pondering the advice of the star-gazing Madame Soleil: cutting out dress patterns from *Elle:* answering in meticulous handwriting the personals published in *Libération*

for example: lone wolf, cast into a dark cell by our odious repressive society, seeks soulmate for lasting friendship and possible matrimony: or: buried as I am at the botttom of a black hole, who will be the gentle friend who will give me the gift of hope by offering me kind words and the bright glow of motherly affection?: or: you, my mythical female reader, hold your hand out to me in a spirit of generosity as I offer you

mine, for if you abhor sadness, believe in brotherhood, yearn for a sincere and faithful companion I
promise I can show you how to rid yourself of your
dark melancholy!: or: blazing sun of human warmth,
a gesture, a look from you through the bars imprison-
ing my spirit drenched in fog and rain will put an end
to my present blindness and give me the strength and
courage to face my wretched existence: or: if you feel
alone and lost, as I do, and nonetheless yearn for
happiness, take your pen in hand, don't hesitate a
moment, your reply will keep us both from sinking
into the hell of a selfish and sinister world: or: drifting on the sea of life, a shipwrecked survivor on a
desert island, a letter, a simple, subtle, magnanimous,
delicate feminine letter would be enough to show me
that salvation is possible, pointing me toward a
beacon of kindliness and hope

they always begin like that: aid, support, companion-
ship, fulfillment, creativity, free fraternal souls: noble
sentiments, pure motives, altruistic tendencies: simple, domestic, earthy tastes: reading, music, photography, travel, breathing fresh country air far from the
city: if you like sun-drenched beaches, the taste of salt
on your lips, soft breezes caressing your hair, here I

am: the man of your dreams!: all to lull you to sleep and make you believe they're not thinking about what they never stop thinking about: but I'm not exactly a babe in the woods, she's been around, she's learned a thing or two over the years and when she reads I'm looking for someone with deep affinities for the arts or a shared interest in the esoteric she knows very well what comes next, the p.s., the dropped hint, what's written between the lines, as they begin to trust you, amid yards of purple prose about a sublime relationship against a background of azure sea and sky, snow-covered peaks, a vast unexplored desert, places lending themselves to the discovery of the immense potential for expression of that stranger with whom you live side by side every day of your life and I alone can awaken, my love: your own body

and once that point has been reached, the moment of truth, H-hour, the rogues let their hair down: their aspirations and desires are not as lofty as they proclaimed them to be: with a thousand stylistic precautions, resorting to the usual repertory of euphemistic formulas, they hint at aptitudes and talents, expertise, consummate skill, mastery: their dream of a woman with no inhibitions or complexes, capable of giving outward expression to their physical and emotional needs in the company of an attentive, obliging, liberated lover (neither a phallocrat nor a traditionalist nor a male chauvinist pig) but rather, gentle, sensual, understanding, mature, tolerant, clever hands, a tongue of silk and velvet, whose stubborn, progressively frenetic perseverance is centered, will be centered, it's his specialty, his hobby, his mania, on that pearly, divine button that is the doorbell, the alarm clock of volcanic feminine sensuality

some clippings from her collection, arranged in an ascending scale of shamelessness
if you are passionate, liberal-minded and curious, physically attractive, don't you need a man with similar gifts with whom you can fulfill your fantasies, with no taboos whatsoever?
whatever your age, tall or short, a blonde a brunette a redhead, if you're a female who likes to fuck nonstop, get in touch with me: you'll be suitably rewarded!
dude seeks torrid chick to set off fiery rocket and explode in the heavens together
tall, strong, virile, well-hung stud offers riding lessons to a hefty filly in heat who's hot to trot
owner of a high-caliber long-barreled rifle wishes to

place it in the hands of a female willing to polish and
grease it before having her temperature taken with it,
from the front and from the back

yes
it's true
I know the two of you as well as if I'd given birth to
you!
years ago, in her militant days, when she believed she
was fighting against alienation, from totally alienated
positions
(you hadn't yet entered my life)
she exchanged letters, you exchanged letters, driven
perhaps by desires both unavowed and unavowable
(settling down, respectability, possible marriage with
dependable, reliable gentleman)
with what turned out to be
(yes, but I can't help laughing anyway!)
a really slippery scoundrel
(it was the romantic, chaste, platonic, spiritual
period of your life)

all right then, I'll tell you the whole story
they were put in touch with each other, you were put

in touch with each other thanks to the services of a matrimonial agency, and he immediately contacted you, by mail, since he lived a long way away, ah if only he could be at your side, in the warmth of the glowing hearth, in our little house, listening to Mozart quartets, Brahms sonatas, you, my beautiful stranger, my dream woman, the refuge from all my cares, the angel of my home and fireside, in a word, letters that couldn't have been more poetic or respectful, a real gentleman, days, weeks, months with no inane drivel whatsoever, all sweetness and light, incredibly beautiful turns of phrase, angel from heaven, love of my soul, my treasure trove of goodness, and she, you, naive and innocent me, taken in like an idiot by his honeyed words, without realizing that slyly, in passing, as though that were not at all his intention, he was beginning to worm his way into my confidence, to show his true colors, taking more and more liberties, imagining her naked, cradled in his arms like a child, still listening to Mozart and Brahms, snuggled up next to each other now, and him rigid, erect, that's my normal state, I don't know if you realize it, but I have a fiery temperament, and when I think about a woman like you, my blood rushes to the spot that you can well imagine, my member stands at attention, it's really outsized, an enormous tool, I'm sending you a photo so that you can see and judge for yourself, a snapshot taken by an intimate lady-friend, tomorrow I'll mail you other full-length photos of me, wearing a mask, I'm the one in the middle of the group, it's always easy to tell which one is me, I'm the one with the biggest cock, what do you think of positions eight, sixteen, thirty-two?, I hope that when you contemplate them they will produce a warm, moist reaction on your part, cause your hand to descend to your darling little button, and discover that your panties are soaking wet, but I was blind, I swear, I continued to perch there on cloud nine without realizing, without noticing that the guy didn't want to marry me or any other female, that he was one of those cold intellectual types that gets his kicks writing all sorts of filthy things, and when she sent him the photograph of herself that he kept insistently requesting, even though she had gone that very day to the electrolysist and despite the fact that you had told the photographer to make sure your Adam's apple, your collar bones, the treacherously revealing length of your arms didn't show, it was quite obviously a studio pose, with an illusion veil and a printed silk dress, he sent me by return mail a registered letter canceling our meeting: a brother of his, that I haven't mentioned to you before, had just been assassinated by guerrilla-fighters of some liberation front or other, in Madagascar or Indochina, I don't remember exactly, and he was obliged to go there immediately, deal with the situation, take care of family matters, impossible to put off, my boat leaves tomorrow, goodbye dreams, hopes, plans, farewell, farewell my love, it's fate that's to blame, we could have been happy together, life itself absurdly sends us on our separate ways

one disappointment after another, but you didn't blink an eye, she continued to peruse the personals columns, to answer letters, and the same record, the same tune, the same song and dance was repeated over and over again, ecology, classical music with febrile overtones, daring proposals that to your utter frustration never quite jelled: she was obliged to flee those precincts where she found herself, run the risk of a complicated, intricate operation, try her luck in rugged, remote environs: the setting of an old love-film was the ideal decor in which the protagonists of her long-standing frustrated deflowering could harmoniously play their roles: real men such as yourself, possessed of rough-and-ready, convincing sex appeal, endowed with a superb, unique, ineluctable tool: someone had told me about you, an incredible infantryman stationed in Targuist, and I wrote to you, with no false hopes this time, like someone throwing an empty bottle with a message into the sea, not yet knowing that despite our differences of class and age, the sentence you were serving, the dizzying accumulation of obstacles, he was, he would be the man in her life, that the two of you, the two of us were fated to love each other

but he was not like the others
you went straight to the point
he answered you, you answered me in a crude, clumsy, thick-stroked hand, your scribe was one of your jailmates, addicted to rigorously phonetic spelling, who inserted parentheses and glosses, invocations of the mercy of Allah, proposals that were his own invention into the text you dictated, asked you to remember him, said that the two of you were like brothers to each other, begged you to be so kind as to send him a slight recompense, a few pesetas so as to be able to buy tobacco, but pleez dont tell him I asked becauz if he fowned out hed be as mad as a wild beest

---

I was working at the time in a musical, at the Teatro
Cervantes, and your letter literally bowled me over
Ive herd a lot about you becuz your a big star and
they say your looking for a man and want to be
formully engajed, do you remember?, and then he
told her he was a corporal, first class, unmarried and
without a family, and sent you a snapshot of himself
taken in an automatic photo booth, in his Regular
Army beret, fierce-looking, dark-skinned, flashy, attractive in a roguish way, a real Moorish lady-killer
with a big bushy mustache, Ive got a nenormous
cock, almost a foot long, it hangs out when I wair my
jim pants and lootenant Garsia calls me a freek of
nature if you kum to see me hear in Targis tell the
sarjent on gard your my fiansay and theyll let me see
you alone and the too of us will have lots of hapines
and plezure together if thats gods will
and he, the scribe
what he sez is trew hes got a nenormously long one
and the captin doesn't let him go to the cathouse hear
in Targis becuz the madam sez she has to send her
gurls to the hosspital afterwurds and when he does
jimnastics he wairs long pants otherwise his tale stiks
out and cauzes a terrible comotion
you didn't tell me why you were in jail, just that i got
put in the slammer for thre munths one day when luk
wasnt going my way, but the scribe, after once again

125

mentioning the business about sending a money
order, shed more light on the subject, he fuked a boy
in the ass, that was the secret you were hiding, you
outlaw, and the padre, on seeing the dammidge hed
dun, denounsed him, and sinse he was a nefew of the
Kaid they listened to him, but it isnt a very searious
charge and theyll let him go free thanx be to god if he
pays the boys family a yearling sheap
the p. s. was scrawled in red ink on a separate sheet of
paper, in a slightly different hand
this is a curl of hare from when I shaved miself down
belo that im sending you becuz ive fallen in love with
your beauti theirs a buss that goes from tanger to
alasema its best to purchiss yur tikket in advanse sinse
its a very small buss and its alwayz crouded

how to resist your urgent, forceful arguments?
mystical, head in the clouds, exultant, she took the
bus
a poky, panting, asthmatic, flatulent crate with rumbling bowels, full to the gunwales with peasant
women swathed in heavy veils, with broad-brimmed
straw hats, tassels, paper streamers, knots of rumpled ribbons, rudimentary merry-go-rounds, amid
baskets, bundles, household goods, scared rabbits,

irate hens, sleeping children, a chaos of voices, shouts, alarming snorts from the engine, ear-splitting cackles, swinging and swaying, sudden applications of the brakes, jolts and shudders, mysterious stops, dizzy spells, vomiting, passengers getting on and off, police checks, large family groups, fights for seats, hallucinatory late-afternoon landscapes, donkeys bearing incredible burdens, flocks of sheep and goats, ravenous field crops, miserable huts, women sitting along the roadside awaiting an unlikely resolution of their fate, horns blasting, packs of mules, people returning home from the marketplace, shepherd boys as motionless as scarecrows, men prostrated in prayer or squatting on their haunches urinating, a hesitant twilight, an indifferent and apathetic light, an anemic sun that had bled copiously, one last violent hemorrhage, an orgiastic death-agony, before setting, sinking, dragging all of you with it to your ruin, orphan plains, wandering shades, gathering darkness, fleeting silhouettes

her face hidden behind a veil too, strictly incognito, wearing no makeup or cosmetics, spared inquisitive, surprised stares from your indecipherable neighbors thanks to their cool reserve and the fact that they are absorbed, luckily, in the silent contemplation of another European passenger, pale, blonde, obese, aerostatic, inflated, ready at any moment, it would appear, to slip her moorings and soar majestically upward like a magnificent hot-air balloon

no, I'm not being malicious, it's the truth and you know it, she harbored no ill-will toward anyone nor was she in the habit of exaggerating, I always try to be fair

she had settled down comfortably in two seats with one buttock on each, I presume she'd paid double fare, in any case the bus driver didn't say a word and everyone treated her with respect: a commanding presence, as imposing, spectacular, immense as a giant protest demonstration, fanning herself, stifling from the heat even though it was the dead of winter, with a minuscule head in relation to the size of her body, dull, bulging eyes, a button nose, a big round mouth pursed in astonishment, she was panting, poor thing, and had to open it and down something liquid, if only she'd exhaled a little stream of bubbles you'd have sworn she was in an aquarium

don't be angry, my love, I'm talking just to hear myself talk as the saying goes, to enliven the evening a bit, to chase the silence away

it was late at night and the bus was zigzagging up the mountain, I remember the bright moonlight in the wadi, frequent stops, flickering lights, wretched silhouettes in djellabahs, a cheap café full of kif-smokers, Bab Berrad, a fragrant glass of mint tea, my head nodding, half asleep despite the fuss being made by a peevish, somnambulant chicken, and more endless twists and turns, still going up and up, a parched plateau, seeming to float amid clouds, sudden brushstrokes of light, dense stands of trees, a vigil of firs, a police checkpoint at Ketama, soldiers from Moroccan units, Legionnaires, arguments, paper-shuffling, searches, the expulsion of an old woman with no identification, on the move again, earrings, potholes, gullies, ferris wheels, rough seas, drifting helplessly, heavy surf, fog, a boxom blonde Valkyrie, a stage setting for The Flying Dutchman

it was just getting light as we arrived at Targuist
it was too early to go see you, she took a room in an inn, you drank a cup of coffee, you made up your face with great care, she had read your letter dozens of times, I knew it by heart, I waited for them to blow reveille, to raise the flag, I was bringing you a sack full of clothes, sweaters knitted especially for you, a bottle of eau de cologne, a pair of gym trunks with tight-

fitting legs so that you could conceal from others' eyes your precise dangling treasure, as happy as a little girl on the day of her first communion as I walk toward the barracks where his regiment is quartered, serene, confident of the truth of your words, not at all impatient, on the contrary, savoring each moment as I wait, immune to flirtatious advances and invitations, radiant, self-assured, circumspect, finally reaching the white battlemented building, little boxes with sentries standing guard, Todo por la Patria, she gave your name to the corporal on duty, you went on into the visitors' room, orderlies, Andalusian privates, a drowsy quartermaster, the second lieutenant hadn't arrived yet, you were obliged to wait with the others, sitting on a stone bench, with your handbag on your knees, reserved, on your best behavior, they'd given you a number, each visitor was called in turn, and I thought of you, my love, the merits that fame attributed to you, the incomparable glory of your exploits

seven!

yes, your number, she rose to her feet, you went to the little dispatch window, handed the cardboard box to the sergeant

he: who is it you want to see?

I, proud of you, in a good loud voice, so that everybody would hear me: Corporal First-Class Azizi

Mohamed, ID number 2846!

he: is he a relative of yours?

I: no, sir, I'm his fiancée

and suddenly, from behind me, the thundering of a stentorian voice, with the irreversibility of sudden catastrophe

vat does she mean his viancée?

the hot-air balloon, still moored to the ground, gasping with astonishment, tilting the little bottle of vodka toward the open circular cavity

you are most zertainly not his viancée, you're a dezpigable impostressss!

she came forward, dragging her tiny feet as she walked, as though afraid she might lose contact with the earth and levitate without the aid of gas

the gorboral iss my lawvully vedded hussbant, ve were marriet by progzy, here are my paperss ant my stemped pessport!

everyone fell silent, smelling tragedy in the air, the sergeant stared at the two of us, suddenly seemed to get all excited, and sent a message to the lieutenant, the other woman puffed and snorted, a gelatinous, piscicolous, medusan blob, furiously waving her Lithuanian passport, she'd crossed all of Europe to see you, I'm going to ingform the conssul of my coungtry, this iss an outrache, and you, my love, enjoying the peace and quiet of your cell, unaware that you had

131

caused a terrible rumpus, a great to-do in the visitors'
room, till the lieutenant sent for you and they
brought you there, escorted by two guards, and once
it dawned on you that there was a dreadful ruckus
going on you tried to back away, you played dumb,
you pretended not to have any idea what the uproar
was all about, it was revolution, all the officers in the
place had formed a circle around the two of you as
though you were a pair of fighting cocks, the Lithuanian heaped abuse on me, screaming at the top of her
lungs, and everyone was vastly enjoying the whole
situation, extending you their congratulations, com-
menting on the international renown of your member, but I remained cool and calm and collected, I'd
seen you now, your dashing, youthful charm, your
imposing bearing, the ample curve of your trousers
fly fulfilled my age-old, long-standing hopes, I knew
that we would meet again, a favorable astral conjunction would reunite us, this slight hitch made me
laugh, I swear, the other woman raved on in her
Baltic accents and you listened, abashed but impeni-
tent, cunning as ever, a splendid mountain lion after
a night of unspeakable whoring around

this Rif bit has been quite a riff and I've forgotten
what I was going to say, must be twenty after or the

devil passing by as the old proverb goes, and you still aren't ready, eyebrow pencil, mascara, rouge, lipstick, eyelashes curling like whips, a touch of black paint for the beauty marks, impossible to tidy up your refuge a bit, photo novels, bundles of faded letters, illustrated magazines, pages of personals, the clipping from years back that led me to seek you out, impelled her to cross the ocean, to land in America, a tool that sends shivers up your spine ladies and gentlemen, the biggest cock in the entire world, a wildly excited eyewitness report describing its dimensions, extolling its size, providing a running commentary on your theatrical apotheosis

bundling yourself up well against the cold, going out into the street, wandering through the city of metal and fog, cars, snowflakes, traffic lights, not even thinking of making a pickup, not even trying the cruising areas, the Greyhound Terminal, Exchange Way, Liberty, Penn Avenue, eagerly following the trail that is to lead to the catacombs, to the sumptuous dark lair, your nuptial chamber, guided only by the fine-tuned instinct of the seer, awaiting a sign from fate, little round pebbles strewn in your wake à la Tom Thumb, caves, the infernal regions, sewers, nocturnal speleology, illuminated by the faith that you inspire in me, cheerful, resolute, persevering, doughty, tireless

SIGHTSEEING TOUR

the vitality of a great melting pot: the imaginative efforts of industrial leaders: a concentration of natural resources and financial wealth: a fortunate geographical formation and location: all of these assets contribute to the character of the present-day city
with the earphones in place, the conventioneers, the delegates, the visitors comfortably settled in their seats, isolated, protected, soundproofed beneath the transparent, convex, vitreous, oblong, heliofiltering roof: a gigantic cetacean seemingly drowsing, its diaphanous, radiant structure magnified by the punc-

134

tual, diligent, almost opportunistic rays of a sun that ordinarily, at this time of year and in these latitudes, is in the habit of offering only the scantiest glimpses of its golden presence and showing its leonine head only after a well-nigh interminable wait, like a prima donna who, after withdrawing from the enthusiastic applause of her fans, finally deigns to step out once again through the curtain drawn across the stage, yielding at long last to the persistent, heartfelt pleas of the audience

here, the pistons of technological development accelerated in the course of the twentieth century and maintained their rhythm even during the Depression years: shafts of steel, sheaths of glass, thrusts of concrete gradually reshaping the contours of the great metropolis: these reflect the spirit of a city founded upon ideas: new concepts with which to experiment, and proven ones to serve as a basis for innovation

explanations, analyses, panegyrics simultaneously translated by the headphones into the native dialect of the medina, into rough vernacular speech: fairgrounds entertainers, habitués of the public square come on a group tour to enjoy the unusual, attractive spectacle of the hustle and bustle, the hurry and scurry, the smog of the distant industrialized metropolis: prudently protected from any possible environmental contamination

(one can never be too cautious in these suspect, un-

135

known lands, so strange and so fascinating)
thanks to the strong, hermetically sealed roof of the
monster chartered through Sahara Tours: absorbed in
contemplation of the picturesque, exotic panorama,
gazing open-mouthed at the local color of inordinate,
oneiric city planning, amazed at the dizzying, indissoluble, motorized, cellular, proliferation
*technological advances are consistently forthcoming from
our industry: nonmanufacturing enterprises currently
thrive and multiply in a most encouraging environment:
all of these efforts and ventures project the city squarely into
the exciting business of anticipating tomorrow: in addition
to supplying many of the materials that are the mainstay of
today's civilization, this capital has commited itself to a
sort of permanent transition, forever seeking imaginative
and resourceful responses to a changing community, nation
and world*
gathered together in the gleaming island of metal and
glass, transported directly from the rose-ocher city:
with their belongings stowed in the ample space provided at the front of the rows of soft reclining seats or
the vast empty space situated underneath the velvety
cushions: a little metal box containing all their
worldly goods, a worn pack of cards, an anatomical
plate in color, a treatise on the art of love and aphrodisiac recipes, an old, well-thumbed copy of the

136

Koran: elderly men dressed in white from head to foot, girls with silver earrings and bracelets, delicate, transparent almaizales, a profusion of new sashes and slippers, turbans like gracefully coiled serpents

it exports steel, aluminum, glass, coal, iron, food products, know-how, and football players: it creates new talent, new ideas, and new industries: it is a city of contrasts: the present is the cornerstone of the future, and the excitement today revolves around the ambitious plans the people have for their community: it is an amazingly young man!: and if our citizens have anything to do with it, he will grow younger and stronger the older he gets!

a simpleminded soul stroking the strings of his rebec, lovinglycradling it like a wet nurse

a veiled woman who tells fortunes

a miracle-monger bending down to draw graffiti with his bit of chalk

a young acrobat dressed in a little short jacket and bright-colored balloon pants

Gnaua dancers, in immaculate trousers and blouses, smooth, dark legs, unadorned and quintessentially naked

a giant with a strong skull shaved perfectly bare, a thick stubby neck, broad shoulders, coppery skin, thick lips, a Mongol mustache trickling down past his chin, gold-capped teeth

an elderly mime decked out in a blond wig
two clowns wearing donkey's ears and rudimentary
disguises
sinewy flute players, with swarthy complexions and
bushy mustaches, accompanied by a transvestite in a
filmy veil, female garments, an embroidered sash
a collector of lizards, with a fawnlike chin beard, like
a splendid billygoat
a public scribe with a pen, an inkwell, and a wrinkled
sheet of parchment
tradesmen, expounders of the Law of Islam, craftsmen, shopboys, students of the Koran
*as you will observe, our reputation as an industrial center
is matched by our growing ability to entertain, to en-
lighten, to provide diversions for all ages and interests:
within a compact city the vacationer, the businessman and
the entire family find easy access to a variety of exceptional
leisure activities*
a confluence of rivers, a superimposition of architects'
models, gleaming metal structures, octagonal sky-
scrapers of tinted glass, steel bridges, a spherical
skullcap like a ring of Saturn or an ecclesiastical zuc-
chetto: listening attentively to the simultaneous
translation by their cicerone, who smiles and carries
his zeal to extremes, awaiting the moment when he
takes them back to the hotel where they are staying

and obsequiously pockets the mezzo-voluntary tip: stressing for this reason the most colorful and most typical aspects of his homeland, details likely to arouse their interest and feed their predictable curiosity: the recently passed municipal ordinance, for instance, forbidding the natives to walk within the city limits, in order to prevent the slow and clumsy gait of bipeds from interfering with free and rapid flow of vehicular traffic: those who break this law are liable to immediate arrest and must undergo a mandatory alcohol test: with a fine payable in situ, and in the case of repeated offenses, the inferior members of the guilty party are subjected to induced atrophy and he is then sent to a free rehabilitation center: adding with a reassuring smile that these measures, while undoubtedly draconian, yet at the same time salutary and just, do not apply in any case to visitors and tourists: we believe in the absolute excellence and validity of our own model: we nonetheless respect others' choices and make no attempt to impose ours on the rest of the world by force

few places on this planet enjoy topographies as spectacular as ours: the city's triangular formation bounded by three rivers, the Allegheny, the Monongahela, and the Ohio, creates an unforgettable visual experience: an observation deck fashioned by nature rises 600 feet above the rivers to

*present an extraordinary 17-mile-wide panorama of the
city: some of our most glamorous restaurants and cocktail lounges are situated atop Mount Washington, and
luncheon or dinner is enhanced by an exciting view: in the
evening, from May through October, an illuminated fountain plays at the Point*

allowing them to focus their binoculars on the jet of
the fountain prodigally ejaculating its plume of futile
foam, to let their gaze linger on the triangular garden, mindful of a pubis, created by the confluence of
the rivers, to exchange wonderstruck comments as
they sit, safely isolated, inside their hermetically
sealed bus

pointing out next other notable and surprising facets
of the industrious city and its unique social system

*people traveling to the city from Parkway West pass
through the Fort Pitt Tunnel and onto the Fort Pitt
Bridge, which constitutes the most impressive gateway to
the downtown area, its span suddenly standing out against
the vertical splendor of the Golden Triangle: the Hilton
Hotel faces the bridge: the buildings of Gateway Center rise
in the background: top right: our oldest structure, the Fort
Pitt Blockhouse, attracts history students to Point State
Park: across the Allegheny River, the Three Rivers Sta-
dium creates a contemporary contrast*

fast-food places, for instance

on walking past one of these establishments, a McDonald's or a Kentucky Fried Chicken, let's say, with its functional plastic stools and tables where the customers are downing hamburgers, hot dogs, or ham sandwiches, separated from those passing by on the street only by the indiscreet half-moon of the big front window, is there anyone who has not had the idea pop into his head to stop in front of one of these dimwitted gluttons cramming food down his gullet and stare at him from the other side of the glass in mute, stern, cold reproof till he is thoroughly disconcerted and embarrassed, exactly as though he were taking a shit?

well, this shocking spectacle, so common in other times, has been completely eradicated in our pioneer city, for the pure and simple reason that we have radically transformed the primitive, traditional conception of food

instead of heavy, indigestible dishes, which pointlessly overload the stomach and in time cause all sorts of intestinal ailments, we have persuaded people to consume only predigested products so as to spare their bodies the wear and tear occasioned by the mastication, deglutition, and assimilation of nutritive materials: our most aggressive promotional slogan: have no fear these days of stomach ulcers or gallbladder complaints or diseases of the pancreas: eat without anxieties or complexes: we have providently predigested for you!

how? through the mass manufacture of pills, soluble capsules, and tablets that for your convenience contain the precise equivalent of vitamins, calories, salts et cetera of the corresponding foods that they handily replace: dissolved slowly in the mouth, they provide your taste buds and your palate with delights capable of satisfying the standards of perfection and refinement of the most exacting gourmet

whether in an ordinary snack bar, a modest luncheonette, or the most exclusive, high-class French restaurant, you may choose the dish or combination of dishes that appeals to you most and enjoy, by youself, with your family, or with employees of your company, depending on your desires and your financial means, either a quick bite or an elaborate three-star banquet

observe, ladies and gentlemen, the restaurant just across the way: a bright young Kauffmann's executive and his wife are celebrating their tenth wedding anniversary and have chosen for the occasion an elegant, discreet, classic décor: waiters in tuxedos, a chef in a white toque, exquisite chinaware, luxurious embroidered table linen: the menu: crème vichyssoise,

soufflé de barbue au coulis d'écrevisse, filet de boeuf
aux truffes, charlotte aux framboises: the ceremony,
the atmosphere, the service, the background music
are the same as always, but the various dishes have
been replaced by tiny concentrated tablets with a
most subtle aroma and a delicate flavor that free the
long-suffering digestive apparatus from its repetitive,
mechanical function: absorbing the meal through
the walls of the intestines or expelling it along sinuous curves and meanders till it reaches the calami-
tous, ill-fated final straight stretch: add to this the
exciting possibility of being able to eliminate any
trace or residue of the ethereal, quintessentified repast
ingested by simply pressing the button that has nobly
replaced the old-fashioned chain and tank in our original patented model of the electronic waterflush com-
mode, and you will be in a position to appreciate the
amazing import, in terms of hygiene and aesthetics,
of our community's bold decision!
*in this compact city a tourist may reach any important
downtown destination by walking if he wishes: on the way,
he may shop at, or simply browse through, the world market of synthetic foods: he may choose from a variety of fine
restaurants, some with breathtaking views of the area: in
planning our changing scene, we consider the well-being of
our citizens and our guests!*

143

another characteristic feature that is ours alone: our
rational, unbeatable system of fecundation
as you doubtless already know, ladies and gentlemen
(an inscrutable expression on the faces of the sight-
seers from Marrakesh packed together like sardines in
the panting cetacean)
the creation of an individual presupposes the union
of two gametes: an ovum and a spermatozoid
there is ordinarily only one of the former: released by
the ovary at the end of each menstrual cycle, its trajectory is a short, simple one: entering the trumpet-
shaped opening of the Fallopian tube and traveling
down the latter to meet its complementaries
these
on the contrary
are ejected by the millions, with a large proportion of
them being defective or sterile
(some forty percent are abnormal in form and in-
fertile)
a somewhat smaller number are incapable of motion
or slow-moving
(between approximately twenty and thirty percent)
along with a great amount of residue
(cells that are immature or not involved in the process of reproduction)
the purpose underlying this enormous disproportion
in the production of male and female gametes con-

stitutes a profound mystery that biologists and scientists all over the world have tried in vain to fathom
the race to the ovum
ladies and gentlemen
more or less calls to mind the image of a gigantic cross-country marathon
at the beginning of the competition, millions of participants, as though in obedience to the starter's whistle, hurtle forward to penetrate the vagina, in which a large majority of them will remain, stopped dead in their tracks, prematurely beaten and exhausted
only a few hundreds of thousands will succeed in entering the liquid secretion at the neck of the uterus, a barrier or impediment that results in a radical initial selection: there those that are incompetent, awkward or sluggish, those that are lazy, those with very little motility will come to grief
those on the other hand that are most active and enterprising will contrive to reach the crypts of the cervix and will set out in successive battalions of several thousands to conquer the coveted gamete of the opposite sign, which only the cleverest, swiftest, strongest one of all will manage to penetrate
in pursuit of this goal they will be obliged to go on with their cross-country marathon and skirt a series of ever-increasing difficulties and more and more perilous traps, on the order of those which lie in wait for

the player who enjoys a lively game of royal goose, but which, unlike the latter, involve in each case the possibility of committing an irreparable, necessarily fatal error

they must traverse the upper part of the uterus, chemically hostile, bristling with dangers, and enter the Fallopian tube, where the risks are fewer and the run momentarily benign, propitious

several hundreds will thus approach, step by step, in an exciting obstacle race, the last section of it, a terrain favorable to fecundation

it is a tremendously stirring moment, ladies and gentlemen!

this heat has lasted approximately six hours and the vast majority of the participants have thrown in the towel, have died of inanition!

the successive waves of runners who have taken off from the cervix will remain in this choice spot for three or four days, a pause taken advantage of by each competitor to perfect his own skill and training and analyze in minute detail the technique and talents of the others

the ovum, as lovely as a blonde fairytale princess, witnesses in solitary splendor the implacable gamesmanship of the rival gametes as they steal fearful glances at each other and watch each other's slightest movements like a hawk, ready to frustrate forthwith

the dreams of conquest on the part of the most impatient or daring of the competitors
the cross-country marathon has insidiously turned into an extraordinary rugby match, the sole rule of which is the struggle to the death of all against all!
free-for-alls, tripping, dribbling, as the anxious spermatozoids, in a mad frenzy now, draw closer and closer to the passionately desired goal!
and at this moment one of them
ladies and gentlemen
nimbly, cleverly, imaginatively, fantastically
makes his way with lightning speed through the pack, avoids the traps they set for him, runs, gives all of them the slip, keeps going, on and on!
incredible, ladies and gentlemen!
the fabulous gamete, the Pelé, the Zatopek, the Di Maggio of spermatozoids definitely outdistances all his competitors!
he covers the stretch that separates him from the ovum in an amazing display of speed and style!
he runs forward, draws closer, closer still, takes his shot, gets it in, gets himself in, hits the target s-q-u-a-r-e i-n t-h-e c-e-n-t-e-r!
GOAL, GOAL, GOAL!!!
an unforgettably exciting moment, ladies and gentlemen: the crowd is cheering itself hoarse!
the one, the only winner among millions of hapless

participants, the hero of the day, the ace of aces is having an absolutely marvelous time with his blonde princess, and with all our heart we wish the two of them

      a most enjoyable dingle-dangle
      a spine-tingling tickle-tackle
      a splendid sucky-fucky
      a fantastically frictious bacon-rubbing
      a sweet-juicy maxigasm

happy honeymoon, you lucky, big-balled superstud!
you won her against all the odds, like a champ!
enjoy yourself, have a ball, turn off your mind, fall ass over teakettle in love!
from the boxes, the grandstands, the bleachers, the spectators, each and every last one of us, envy you!

this Gateway Center skyscraper wears its skeleton of high-strength special alloy steel on the outside: it is the head-quarters for the United Steelworkers of America

the most recent addition to the Gateway complex is the world headquarters building of Westinghouse Electric Corporation

let us now turn our attention to the exceptional geo-logical configuration of our industrious city
from the magnificent natural observation deck of Mount Washington, the wedge or space that gradu-ally tapers to a point as the Allegheny and Monon-

gahela rivers converge, their mingled waters forming
the majestic Ohio River

the apex of this inverted triangle is situated in Point
State Park: from there its sides little by little broaden
out, breasting the waters of the two rivers as they
flow downstream

might not our beloved, world-famous Golden Triangle thus be said, perhaps, to resemble a graphic
representation of the female organs of reproduction
in the course of the menstrual cycle?

examine next, ladies and gentlemen, the anatomical
plate projected on the closed television circuit inside
the bus: we are certain that this proof of the extraordinary parallel that we have suggested will astound
you!

does not the green garden of Point State Park call to
mind the pleasing, welcoming setting of that coveted
contrivance known as the vagina?

let us now shift our gaze to the point through which
thousands upon thousands of vehicles coming from
Fort Pitt Tunnel pour into the city in an endless
stream, heading up the artery known as Liberty Avenue, stretching from the modern buildings of the
Hilton Hotel complex to the State Office

this point of entry, which, alas, is all too frequently
the site of obstructions and traffic jams, the inevitable

product of its characteristic funnel shape
is nothing more nor less, as you have already doubtless guessed, ladies and gentlemen
than the neck of the uterus
the uterus itself, often compared to an inverted flattened pear, its lower end being conical and its upper
end broad, squat, and roomy, its sinuous, slightly
concave external walls forming a continuous arcade
from the isthmus of the womb to the point of attach-
ment of the oviducts, the ovary and the round ligament, corresponds, as is obvious, to our celebrated
Business District, within which the most suitable
itinerary for the comprehension of the parallel that
we are tracing would be to start at Liberty, continue
on along Sixth Avenue and Mellon Square, walk past
the imposing masses of stone or steel of the William
Penn Hotel, Carlton House, and the US Steel Building and head up Webster Avenue
that is to say, up the Fallopian tube
a conduit situated on either side of the uterus, on the
upper surface of the broad ligament, connected at one
end to the neck of the womb and at the other to the
ovary, and whose lower isthmus doubles in diameter
at the point where fecundation takes place
a point at which the ovum, after its brief trajectory through the flaring funnel-like opening of the
oviduct, flirtatiously sallies forth to meet the sper-

matozoid point platoon advancing swiftly from the opposite direction

a green zone fortunately provided in the center of the city, a handy arena for the great love-battle, the dreamed-of eiderdown of a thousand engagements, an impressive round bed!

yes, yes, yes

the star in person, stepping into the spotlight!

the captivating, bewitching female gamete, visible at a distance of more than thirty miles thanks to the gleaming stainless steel dome in which the Pennsylvania sun is mirrored

our favorite place of assembly, commemoration, and recreation

the extremely popular

spectacular

ball-grabbing

CIVIC ARENA!

let us imagine the race now, ladies and gentlemen

the mind-boggling obstacle course

the fierce, pitiless cross-country marathon

millions of anxious spermatozoids rush in successive waves across the Fort Pitt Bridge located just at the foot of our marvelous natural observation deck

they enter Point State Park, the pleasant, hospitable vagina

the majority of them will be immobilized in the latter

151

or will come to grief at the Liberty barrier-bottleneck, in a cruel, monstrous hecatomb
but the most capable of them will get around the uterine impediments and dangers, cross the Business District, reach the lower isthmus of the Fallopian tube via Webster Avenue
and there, ladies and gentlemen
the competition becomes a giant rugby match, a fearsome nest of scorpions, a sudden and colossal free-for-all!
the wondrous cupola of the female gamete, our splendid, inimitable Civic Arena fans to a white-hot heat the frantic desires of possession of the host of impassioned rivals!
until one of them, ladies and gentlemen
a Pelé, a Zatopek, and a Joe Di Maggio rolled into one
dribbles his way through the other players, escapes their eagle-eyed vigilance, rushes, runs, dashes toward the ovum at a fantastic pace, meets up with it in a dizzying burst of speed, perforates the steel dome with his powerful drill!
The United States Steel Building is sheathed in Cor-Ten, the corporation's special steel that weathers to form its own protective coating: the 64-story structure incorporates pace-setting engineering innovations and includes a rooftop restaurant with a city-wide view

let us pass now, ladies and gentlemen, from science fiction to the facts

if we keep in mind that the progress that has been made in the field of the preservation of sperm allows us to offer all sorts of procreative alternatives to the couple, provided, of course, that the woman is fertile, why not aim from the very start, we said to ourselves, at the best possible solution?

modern industrial societies are increasingly abandoning the hazardous, clumsy, old-fashioned craft techniques of copulation in favor of a rational and scientific insemination made possible by the existence of sperm banks in which semen is preserved in accordance with the most technically advanced, up-to-date methods of freezing

once stored in tiny tubes measuring 0.5 to 1 millimeter in diameter to which the proper amount of glycerine has been added, whereupon the tubes are immersed in a bath of liquid nitrogen and kept at a constant temperature of −184 degrees, the spermatozoids remain fertile not just for a few hours or days, but for a period of several years: the thawing takes place at room temperature, with no special technique being required: the viability of the sperm diminishes slightly, but an increase in the quantity employed suffices to ensure fertilization: the resulting offspring are physiologically and psychologically normal, and subsequent studies demonstrate conclusively that they occupy privileged positions in all branches of sports, administration, learning

the selection of the donor must be made, as is only logical, in accordance with a series of vital criteria, in order that the child will not possess traits that are incompatible with those of its parents: all donors must be intelligent and healthy, free of any sort of hereditary defect whatsoever, and endowed with sperm of excellent quality

in order to choose the best candidate in the most expeditious and efficient manner, our municipality has hit upon an ingenious procedure that once again is mindful of the cross-country marathon that we have just described: all individuals of the male sex who have reached the age of twenty-one and are possessed of a proper racial background and family ancestry have the right and the duty to participate in the annual competition destined to crown the king of come, the lucky and popular champion stud jackass

the first screening of those who aspire to this title takes place with the aid of computers: a barrier or hurdle that eliminates those who are least fit, as well as immobile gametes introduced within the vaginal nucleus

after thus sorting out the most capable, the process of

narrowing down the remaining candidates is undertaken with the direct participation en masse of those most interested in the matter, *i.e.,* all those widows, married women, and old maids who, after having consulted with the proper legal, religious, and social authorities, desire to have or to repeat the intimate experience of maternity

images in color of hundreds or thousands of suitors are projected via a special television circuit: scenes filmed in the candidate's home, at his place of employment, or in his leisure time, including close-ups of his private parts and most highly personal attributes, in normal conditions or just about to fire off

with all these criteria of judgment in hand, the future mothers now proceed to choose the most dynamic and attractive contenders, assigning each of them a score corresponding to their various qualities and attributes

the winner of this contest is the one earning the highest cumulative score, and having been thus elected by the popular vote of nubile virgins, wives, and mothers of families, he becomes the exclusive fecundator of all the ova of the city by virtue of his privileged, illustrious status as MISTER LOVE!

two octagonal towers with a common core which at once conserves energy and includes the life-safety system of tomor-

155

*row: at right, the ultramodern National Bank Building
and One Oliver Plaza reach for the skies of the future*
a short documentary film on the most recent winner
of the competition
brief sequences of Mister Love with his poodle, elec-
torally patting a baby on the head, decked out in
cowboy attire smoking a Marlboro, lolling on the
beach with a half-consumed bottle of beer
clear, succinct, categorical statements that allow his
listeners to appreciate the warm, passionate, virile
timbre of his voice
I like Heineken's because it tastes good!
an illustrative compendium of his predilections, pref-
erences, favorite reading, philosophical ideas, eating
habits
the perfect outfit?
shirt by Saint-Laurent, pants by Cerruti, jacket from
Barney's, Yanko's soft, flexible, sporty, anatomical
shoes that allow your feet to breathe
what's your ideal woman like: mother, sister, friend,
pal, whore, wife?
a gleaming toothpaste-ad smile in reply
I find all of them tremendously attractive!
closeup of his tool, first flaccid and then erect
his comment immediately thereafter, expressed in
modest, ineffable tones

quite frankly, I haven't had any complaints from anybody!

and again his house, the garden, the swimming pool, at the wheel of his recently acquired Mercury Capri, shopping at Chatham Center, at a meeting of Koppers executives, depositing a check in his personal account at Equibank, handing out smiles and autographs to his future love-partners

his distinguishing traits

> a contagious friendliness
>
> a serene mind
>
> a happy disposition
>
> an iron constitution
>
> an unparalleled wealth of experience
>
> an irresistible personality

an off-camera recap in a female voice

once you try him, you'll always use him!

the retractable stainless steel dome of the Civic Arena and Exhibit Hall is 415 feet in diameter and 135 feet at its apex: the Arena serves as a sports center during the hockey, tennis and college basketball seasons: ice shows, industrial exhibits and musical events of many kinds are also presented here

and now, as the grand finale, ladies and gentlemen, have a look at the unforgettable ceremony of fertilization

the blonde beauty, attractively dressed in white, read-
ies herself to insert the winner's spermatozoid in her
Fallopian tube by means of a catheter
a fluffy hairdo, set in waves, like the top of a vanilla
ice cream cone: patriotic, presbyterian, antisegregationist, abrahamlincolnesque blue eyes: meticulously
outlined red lips of a pinup girl or a fashion model: a
living example of the basic civic virtues of the Pilgrims: abstemiousness, frugality, a firm belief in the
merits of fair play, progress, individualism
photographs of the idol cover the walls and perch on
top of various pieces of furniture in the room, his
enlarged image projected on the screen of the latest-
model television set beams forth a dazzling smile
discreet, romantic background music, intended to
emphasize the transcendent importance and sublime
nature of this meeting
selections from Chopin, Liszt, Johann Strauss accompany the passage from the vagina to the oviduct,
from the Fort Pitt Bridge to the Civic Arena
flushed cheeks, emotion, a look of ecstasy on the face
of the fecundee, which, as you can see with your own
eyes, tenses, becomes contorted: her eyes roll, she
goes into extraordinary paroxysms, shouts, screams,
bellows, howls, with piercing intensity
the spermatozoid
meanwhile

runs forward, draws closer, closer still, takes his shot, gets it in,
gets himself in, hits the target square in the center! bam, that's it!
the strains of the wedding march celebrate the meteor's exploit, the uncontainable explosion of happiness of the ovum's possessor
the ceremony has lasted precisely one minute and thirty seconds by the stopwatch
an unbelievable saving in money, talent, and energy!
for the community
for the contracting parties
for everyone
our motto is the same as always and we shall never tire of repeating it
TIME IS MONEY!
city of hills, valleys, creeks, and three rivers, our capital is laced together with bridges: seven spans can be seen in this fantastic view from Mount Washington
the sightseeing tour has ended
with the earphones in place, the conventioneers, visitors, delegates comfortably settled in their seats, isolated, protected, soundproofed beneath the transparent, convex, vitreous, oblong, heliofiltering roof of the still-drowsing cetacean digest as best they can the explanations, analyses, panegyrics just translated into the native dialect of the medina, the rough ver-

nacular speech: absorbed in contemplation of the picturesque, exotic panorama, gazing open-mouthed at the local color of inordinate, oneiric city planning, amazed at the dizzying, indissoluble, cellular proliferation of automotive vehicles

attractive suburban communities and shopping malls dot roads east from the Golden Triangle: farther east, the Laurel Mountains offer a source of scenic beauty and serve as the location for winter and summer resorts and recreation

when the prodigious whale starts up, the fairgrounds entertainers and habitués of the plaza murmur a wonderstruck ya latif!

the monster swiftly descends the insanely steep slope, suddenly takes off across Fort Pitt Bridge, follows the road leading off through Point State Park, stops with its loads of VIPs in front of the swankiest hotel in the city

standing at the door with his hand stretched out, the obsequious cicerone aggressively reminds the group of his tip

once outside the bus, they are surrounded by the usual curious throng asking for autographs and coins, proposing excursions and sightseeing trips, persistently hawking all sorts of souvenirs

the dazed travelers finally give in out of sheer exhaustion, cross the vast, luxurious lobby of the hotel, receive their room keys from an impassive cerberus, listen to a few last instructions from their mentor, enter the weightless, silent elevators, scatter down the corridors to end their exciting day with PB News, Radio Liberty, sitting in front of the little television screen

HELOISE AND ABELARD

a real scoop: life underground: somebody had told them about it, I don't remember if it was Bob or Bob's brother-in-law, he was driving through the Business District early one morning and saw them lifting the metal manhole cover from the inside, very cautiously he explained, so as not to be discovered, and at first he thought he must be dreaming and parked his car on the corner, turned the headlights off, noted that the cover was still raised, and then saw a head slowly emerge, take a quick look around, and then, after making sure that the place was deserted, the figure pushed the cover to one side, climbed up the last rungs of the ladder inside, gave a whistle to indicate that the coast was clear and five or six more appeared, all of them resembling the first one, a bunch of drunks or beggars, stealing out of their secret hideout to rustle up some food, rummage in the trash cans before the municipal garbage trucks came by, panhandle the few pennies necessary to buy a couple of bottles of cheap wine or rotgut brandy, like nocturnal hyenas on the prowl, I couldn't believe my eyes, I swear, and the same thing happened every night, he knew exactly where, you guys who work at PB News ought to go with him and he'll show you their lair, a little journey through the sewers where they've hidden out, if you slip them a little dough they may let you interview them, can't you just see the title of the broadcast?, The New Troglodytes, In the Subsoil of the Golden Triangle, or better yet, A Day in Avernus, no, that sounds too literary, the radio listeners wouldn't understand, why not something more sensational, spectacular, such as In the Bowels of Our City, hey Joe, what do you think of that for a title?, and he, you're always building houses from the roof down, the title can wait till later, the first thing to do is locate the manhole they use to get inside the sewer system and bring some good portable equipment with us, go see Eddy right away and tell him to give you the best he's got, and not wreck the whole thing for us the way he did last time with his goddamn stinginess, I want something really good, in perfect condition, go on, what are you waiting for?, for you to tell me when you want it for, when the fuck do you think?, we're going down there this very night, baby, listen, I've got a date with a chick, man, you give me a pain in the ass, if you don't want to go with me don't go and that'll be that, but damn it all can't you get it through your thick skull that we've got to get on the ball right away, the guy's a real blabbermouth and seeing as how he's told Bob he'll tell other people, don't you realize that this is big news, that some sonofabitch might get there ahead of us? just a couple of days ago the boss told me straight out, what's needed around here is a little initiative and some new ideas and either you guys come up with some fresh stuff or I'll throw the whole lot of you out on your ear, this isn't a charitable institution, it's a business, and it's one that's got to pay off, is that clear?, so get your asses in gear and bring me something that's never been done before or you've had it, you turds, this is my last warning, that's exactly what he said, kid, those are his very words, so stop busting my balls with that bit about a date with your girlfriend, man, if we don't run after the rabbit we're never going to catch it, this is our big chance, don't you see that?, okay, okay, I'll break my date, I'm coming with you, I'll go right now and arrange for the right equipment, we need something very lightweight, and ropes, knapsacks, lanterns, as though we were speleologists, see what I mean?, sure, but what's up?, have you thought of something?, yeah, Ben, the title, the fucking title, I've got it, it's a lulu, like that kiddie show on TV, do you follow me?, what show?, you sure are thick between the ears, pal, there isn't a snot-nosed brat alive that doesn't watch it, the Jules Verne thing, you dumbhead, Journey to the Center of the Earth

waiting for dark to raise the manhole cover with all the caution that the occasion calls for: the vertical shaft used by maintenance crews, with metal rungs fastened to the side, like the fire escapes of old buildings: starting the descent, after having beamed their pocket flashlights down the shaft to explore the trajectory, carrying the sound equipment on their backs and wearing sewer workers' rubber hip boots: closing the metal trapdoor above their heads after them and

cautiously setting out for the black den in which the
community has installed itself
are you at the bottom yet, Ben?
no, but almost
what's down there?
don't be frightened, my darling, I'm here with you
you and your fucking jokes
think of the fucking success, we'll be famous!
all I asked you was whether you're at the bottom yet
yep, kid, I'm there, no sweat, you'll see!
turning on the tape recorder, making sure the microphone is working properly, clearing his throat, testing the sound
one two three four, last one down gets screwed by a
whore, haha, is it picking up okay?
yeah, loud and clear
and if you'd stay quiet while I'm recording instead of
scratching your nuts it'd pick up even better
come on, shut up and record
>one two three, Journey to the Center of the
>Earth, In the Catacombs of Our City, a world-
>wide exclusive by PB News, Candid Micro-
>phone, Second Program!
a long passageway sloping abruptly downward, scurrying rats, the murmur of flowing water, mysterious
symbols scratched on the walls, traces proving that

human beings once assembled here: candle ends, empty wine bottles, paper sacks from a liquor store or grocery, a copy of the day's local newspaper, a battered beer can: the flashlight beam suddenly breaks up synods of rodents: rusty pipes run along the passageway, smoking like fireplace chimneys here and there

did you see that, Ben, what do you suppose they're for?

central heating, stupid, don't you realize what the temperature is outside?, these people live underground for the same reasons prehistoric cavemen did, to get out of the cold and survive without having to pay heating bills

reaching the end of the passageway, finding a walkway running along the edge of a vast sewer duct, proceeding along it for a hundred yards or so, suddenly encountering a malodorous waterfall, going up to another level by climbing up a little ladder, finding another walkway, following it along the edge of the cloaca

ladies and gentlemen, all you radio listeners, Joe Brown and Ben Hughes, roving reporters for PB News, in a tape-recorded broadcast from underground, directly below the Business District: Journey to the Center of the Earth!

167

in the bowels of this city, buried beneath the incandescent lava flows of a new Vesuvius, a labyrinth of ladders, passageways, ducts, blind sewers has been the place chosen by a group of our fellow citizens who, disenchanted with the world in which we live, for reasons that they themselves will endeavor to explain in the course of this sensational program, have resolved to take refuge in the kingdom of perpetual night, amid the detritus and excrement that we expel daily, with no other company save that of thousands upon thousands of rodents which, surprised by the unexpected visit of the PB News team made up of myself and my colleague Joe Brown, are fleeing in terror in all directions, isn't that right, Joe?

absolutely, Ben, a spectacle that is enough to kill the prestige of the mighty rat-extermination industry!

our troglodytes have preferred darkness to light, filth to cleanliness, the rodent to the human, a choice difficult to understand, ladies and gentlemen, but one for which the special team from PB News will attempt to provide a plausible explanation with the collaboration of the interested parties themselves

the myth of the cave, the return to the womb,

eh Ben? what would you think of inviting Freud to come down here?

yes, ladies and gentlemen, my friend Joe here is right, our discovery would doubtless have fascinated the celebrated Dr. Edmund Freud if the poor man hadn't died many years ago, the return to the fetal period along with the unconscious attraction of the sewer!, these and many other astounding revelations will be brought to you if you keep tuned in tonight to Joe Brown and Ben Hughes, of the special team from PB News, in its stupendous broadcast: Journey to the Center of the Earth!

is the mike off, Ben?

yeah

well, if you don't mind my saying so, it's pretty obvious that you haven't even read the covers of Freud's works, otherwise you'd know his name wasn't Edmund but Sigmund!

okay, Sigmund, Edmund, whatever, stop bugging me about petty details, this is a program to entertain the general public, angel, not the Friday Evening Culture Digest!

and proceeding along the walkway, accompanied by the roar of linkup pipes emptying into the main sewer conduit, eagerly searching for the trail that will lead them to the troglodytes, but discovering nothing except more conduits, cesspools, walkways, hordes of rats

listen, this is more than anybody could stand, why didn't we bring gas masks?

shut your trap, sweetie, if you don't like it you can blow it out your ass, we've come down here to work, not to sniff jasmine in bloom, okay?

when I think of the date I had up there

well, bring your princess along next time and stop bugging me, who knows, the sight of rats might get her all excited, I know a chick who used to come the minute she spotted one!

bitter jokes, heated exchanges, insults, explosions of wrath: gradually overwhelmed as time passes by the gloom, the darkness, the silence, the feeling of claustrophobia: the maze of ducts, boilers, passageways, pitfalls: the walkway that goes on and on, endlessly: their solitude of miners trapped deep underground, far from the main shaft

discovering with jubilation evidence of an embryonic communal life abruptly abandoned: cigarette butts, tin cans, beds consisting of burlap sacks and cardboard: portable stoves still warm to the touch: a potful of soup half cooked!: like a recently deserted Indian camp

look, Joe, they can't have left more than a minute ago!

170

they must have seen the light, they probably think
we're cops
do you think so?
if not, why would they have taken off like that? listen,
turn the mike on, I'm going to reel off some more
crap, are you ready?
go, man, go!

after an impressive journey through our vast
network of sewers, escorted by a faithful retinue
of good-sized rats and enveloped in a stench
that would make a great number of our good
radio listeners faint dead away, roving reporters
Joe Brown and Ben Hughes of PB News have
discovered the first refuge of troglodytes in the
bowels of our city, directly below Equibank and
Midtown Towers!, the beam of my colleague's
flashlight is picking out at this very moment,
ladies and gentlemen, half a dozen cardboard
cartons flattened out for use as a bed and burlap
sacks serving as pillows, a number of empty
wine bottles, one two three four five beer cans,
a boy-scout knife, a spoon without a handle,
and as incontrovertible proof of their presence
nearby, a can of Campbell's soup still smoking
on the fire, a can of, Joe?
lobster bisque!
a can of lobster bisque, ladies and gentlemen,

171

an incredible success, a stupefying success on the part of the world-famous Campbell Soup Company, whose irresistible expansion knows no limits and has even reached, as we have just seen, these Dantesque precincts!, anything more, Joe?

a receptacle containing water dripping down from the system of heating ducts, a receptacle full of, I'm going to see, I'm putting my hand in it very cautiously so as not to run the risk of getting burned, no, it's not scalding hot, it's lukewarm, full of, let's see here, full of dirty clothes! shirts, two shirts, undershorts, a pair of pants!, a sort of municipal laundry, with two boxes of Tide and even a brush to scrub the most stubborn stains!

fantastic, Joe, really fantastic, the PB News team, in its exclusive program Journey to the Center of the Earth, being broadcast from three hundred feet underground, has unearthed for you, directly below Oliver, Bigelow, and Mellon Square, a rudimentary but flourishing community of fellow citizens who of their own free will have chosen not to embrace our philosophical principles of productivity and progress and instead are reconstructing in the eternal darkness of the catacombs an atavistic, ahistorical, atemporal social structure, in which the solar cycle, the basis of the calendar of all known civilizations to date plays, and this is absolutely extraordinary, no role whatsoever, you were about to say something, Joe?

yes, Ben, follow the beam of my flashlight, the brick, the paving block, the wooden plank are a rudimentary pressing machine used by the troglodytes once they've washed their clothes, and here's proof, a very old pair of soldier's trousers, full of mends and patches yet ironed flat as a board, without a single wrinkle, and perfectly creased!

it is extremely thought-provoking, dear radio listeners, to discover a longing for cleanliness in the inhospitable blackness of these environs, as deeply touching as a ray of light, hope, and tenderness revealing to us that even though their many misfortunes and personal tragedies may have led them to the sad decision to bury themselves alive our brothers of the sewers have nonetheless retained a dim memory of, and mayhap an unavowed nostalgia for their former way of life, when they experienced the drama and the beauty of existence to the fullest just as we do, and at this point I would like to tell you a very simple, very human, very moving story dating back to the time when I was a cub reporter years ago in the ghetto district of the Bronx, but I see that my colleague is motioning me to be quiet, he's doubtless on the track of something very important, and so I'll have to leave my story untold for the moment, ladies and gentlemen, you're listening to Joe Brown and Ben Hughes of the PB News Second Program, back to you in a few minutes!

it was her, it's me, it's you, you were a long time coming, I was beside myself with impatience having to put up with those fools: still dressed in your wedding finery: a romantic flower-print dress with an unconventional low-cut neckline, a full skirt with a ruffled train?: or a combination of the Icarus model, in polyester crêpe de Chine and Étincelle, with a veil and an exquisitely embroidered headband?: in any case smoothing the tulle headdress, not listening to the murmurs of disapproval, the sly whispers, the stifled giggles: commanding attention thanks to your unusual presence alone: invulnerable after your lustral bath in stygian waters: gracefully enveloped in

174

a diaphanous semantic aureole: making your way through the labyrinth with a paschal candle in your hand: a phantasm an apparition a sacred image: preceded, flanked, followed by her prolific court of miracles: rats, mice, little mousies gathered round the moving bubble of light: irresistibly attracted by your somnambulant beauty: unconsciously parodying the expressions and gestures of the all-powerful head of the Secretariat in her brief and capricious levitations in the presence of little shepherds of rugged mountain regions lacking educational facilities: those seraphic poses, fresh from the beauty parlor with her Cartier nimbus-tiara carefully arranged, before lapsing into one of her usual fits of hysteria and hostility, demanding further acts of hyperdulia, allowing herself to be fawned upon by favorites and sycophants: a Madonna in a word, Queen and Lady of the sewers: attracted by your powerful magnet, proudly enthralled by your sovereign plenitude: the flowering staff guides you, your valences will be united, the voltaic arc will joyously spark forth: the solitude will be propitious to our idyll, heraldic mice will be your witnesses, will lead you with exquisite courtesy to the rigors of the nuptial bed: I know that you are as anxious as I am: you remember me as I was when you saw me for the first time, in a remote garrison in the

Magreb, many long years ago: I was a pretty, ingenuous creature then, wandering aimlessly about the world, pursuing no goal, no ideal, but in your absence I have acquired the diabolical skill of an old woman to compensate for the innocence and freshness that I have lost: your delectable flow of honey will comfort me, will restore my lost youth like the plasma of those heedless damsels that the research scientist injected into his hapless châtelaine: oh, how young she is: patience, my darling, I'm going to draw out all her blood!: what an exciting movie!: we saw it in a neighborhood theater, I don't remember whether it was in Uxda or Oran, we were in the last row of seats and the minute you sat yourself down you unbuttoned your pants, he showed her his huge broadsword, he forced her to fondle it, he wanted me to put the whole thing in my mouth, impossible, she gagged, she was not yet an expert sword-swallower at the time, she hadn't practiced breathing techniques, she didn't know how to relax the muscles of her throat properly, you got angry with me, you had put a newspaper over my head so people wouldn't see us and he sat there unconcernedly crunching sunflower seeds, leaving her panting for air, you choked, several times I thought I was about to die of asphyxiation, but you got what you wanted, you rascal, you generously fecundated my gullet, and when he took the newspaper away and let her go, she had tears in her eyes and her nose was running, and she was happy, I swear, I've never seen anything like it in my life, and you decided to learn, to earn your doctor's degree, to exercise your vocal cords like a chorus girl gone mad, to follow a rigorous regimen of gargling, we'd made a date for the following Saturday and I spent the week doing yoga, your serum had given me strength, it was her Siegfried-bath, she rushed to the movie theater all excited, you wanted to show him the progress you'd made, your astounding new talents, and you didn't show up, you bastard, I waited, she waited all afternoon, full of terrible presentiments, you went to the barracks, I asked for you, nobody had any idea where you were, you tried again a number of times, she went to the Cine Mabruka as though it were the votive altar of a cathedral, you had vanished in thin air, it was as if it had all been a dream

recognizing, with pleasure and a sense of relief, the simple, cherished objects in your lodgings: settling yourself comfortably amid them, lulled by the gentle murmur of the stream peacefully flowing through the sewer: unhurriedly stroking his livestock: pro-

177

ceeding to give each of them their fair share of the
booty and contemplating the activity of their incisọrs
with lingering delight: at your ease in the warm hospitality of the bed, surrounded by their solicitous
attentions and flattery, allowing them to run freely
over his body, to nose about as they pleased amid his
members and extremities: feet, head, hands, a naturally prominent organ that is the involuntary cause
of panic, envy, stupefaction: nocturnal, lucifugous,
claustrophiliac, cryptopathic: happy many feet below
ground, after years and years of apprenticeship as an
unsociable creature: separated from the European
workers from the moment you were taken on at the
mine: excluded a priori from all contact with the
outside world: deposits, slag heaps, ore washing
troughs, ventilators for them: toi viens ici, le bicot!:
tu as la chance de ne pas te salir, tu es encore plus noir
que le charbon!: descending to the bottom of the
shaft in the miners' cage, joining the other prisoners
in the galleries: deafened by the rumble of the coal
wagons, the clanging of the steam shovels, the frantic
hammering as the timbers go up: equipped with a
hard hat, a pick, a lantern, a compressed air drill, a
crude and useless alarm device: not realizing that no
one can escape the hand of fate, that one's last hour
has been decreed beforehand!: wriggling through

178

narrow holes, crawling on your hands and knees, working bent over double, envying the deftness and dexterity of subterranean species: I was duped, they duped you: was this the paradise described in the hiring halls, the remunerative work in conditions of freedom within the radiant core of culture?: crouching over to extract hundreds of kilos of coal a day, with the dust and grime stubbornly clinging to your skin despite the sponge, the soap, the purifying shock of the shower water?: pas la peine de frotter ta gueule de bougnoul, tu demeureras toujours aussi sale!: from one mine to another, perpetually buried alive: an ant, a worm, a digging mammal: without the relief of a miserable escape on Sundays like the other immigrant workers: invariably rousing pity and scorn as you pass: did you see that, mama?: for heaven's sake, don't stare like that!: I can't believe it!: can't you see you're embarrassing that man, darling?: don't stand there gaping like an idiot, I tell you: what's he got on his face?: shut up, not another word out of you! he's walking like a robot!: do you think he's crazy?: don't talk so loud, he might attack you!: a scene repeated every time you emerge into the light, an actor against your will in a horror film: obliging those coming in the other direction to step aside, gazing at me in astonishment as they pass by me and turning their heads with expressions of loathing and apprehension on their faces: walking on without seeing them, but knowing that they're staring at you: a burning sensation that runs up my back and suddenly seems to focus itself in the nape of my neck: anxiously seeking anonymity, taking refuge in a movie theater, ending up being lonely for the sedative darkness of the mine: slipping through the hole with the lamp and your work tools, and once out of reach of the foreman, gloriously free from orders and advice, improvising a bed in the rathole, turning the lantern off, resting, escaping, peacefully dreaming with my eyes open: hours of bliss buried in the blackness of the earth, indifferent to the distant din of the machines in the gallery: your one and only regret being, as you look back on it, that intelligent and affable rodents, hoping perhaps to be forgiven for their gluttonous fondness of the cartilage of outer ears, did not come running as they do now to keep you company: dunes, palm trees, grazing cattle, the young girl with the eyes of a gazelle whom you'll one day marry: singing, music, invitations, wedding gifts, three days shut up in the jaima with the damsel, a handkerchief soaked in the blood of her deflowering, jubilant cries from the womenfolk, making love to her, making love to each other all through the fes-

tivities: uach ka-idurrek bissaf?: and she, the young
girl: la, ghir chi chuya, rtaḥ ḥdaya, bghit nnaas maák,
ana ferḥana!: until the pull on the rope jolts me,
drags you away from your eden, forces him to emerge
from his delicious drowsiness: hey, what the fuck are
you doing in there?: did you come down here to take
an afternoon snooze or to work the way you're supposed to? and I: no, boss, I'm piling earth up in a
corner, it's a tough seam to get at, I have to dig some
more with the pick before I can use the drill: apparently kowtowing to him, imitating the refined speech
of the model slave, pretending that your own desires
are identical with the remote interests of Euro-
sucksiety: and once the thundershower is over and
the foreman has gone away, lying down again, seeking bliss in the dark, taking your pleasure once more:
relaxing, stretching, stimulating the girl's nubile
body, setting to rest her fears as to the size of your
member, keeping it hidden so as not to terrify her,
carefully anointing her smooth-shaven pubis, pouring oil into the pretty orifice of her vagina, discreetly
lubricating your own tool: lying down next to her
with all your clothes on, introducing the tip of it into
the half-open slit little by little, smothering her gestures and expressions of anxiety with hungry kisses,
sipping her salty tears with infinite love, applying

pressure as cautiously as a surgeon operating without anesthesia, deepening, widening, putting it farther and farther inside: hey, you, Ears, still sleeping?: my lamp just went out, boss, I was looking for the spare battery: in reality rolling with expert fingers the fragrant hashish joint that he is in the habit of smoking to make his evenings more enjoyable: ready to savor to the fullest the modest but delightful pleasures that life has to offer him: the object of the obsequious celebration of the Muridae gathered round the charismatic erection: fondling, fawning, caresses lavished with tireless diligence by tiny, rough carpet-tongues: lulled by the quiet murmur of the waters, warmed by the emanations of a most efficient system of heating ducts, savoring my own inalienable share of happiness: contemplating amid the ecstasy of their tiny repeated strokings the luminous bubble advancing silently along the gallery: delicate, weightless, phantasmal, radiant, exquisite: a chastely clad silhouette, swathed in tulle like a bride: the object of the worshipful adoration of dozens of mice escorting her on her journey along the water's edge and appearing to kiss her satin slippers as though rendering her the homage that is her due: all the light and beauty of the world ciphered in a face that he divines to be soft and white, modestly hidden behind her filmy veil: the svelte, supple body of a young girl, slender waist, round hips, vernal breasts, delicate hands, delectably tiny feet: coming closer and closer to you, with the paschal candle in her hand, as though on her way to visit Mulay Brahim to pray for a rich and handsome husband, possessed of sound judgment, a kind heart, generous and noble sentiments: the sovereign of a great court of rodents, as majestic and ecstatic as an apparition, her eyes eagerly devouring you before she prostrates herself at your feet like a queen consort at her coronation, overwhelmed by the solemn grandeur of the moment

come closer, darling, let me have a look at you, your presence is dazzling, you're as young and strong as ever, the Almighty is protecting you, you never change, you haven't changed, come here to me, I've missed you terribly, I've searched for you desperately, day and night, snuggle up closer, let me feel you, I can tell you have an erection, your scepter, your gnarled pilgrim's staff, my marshal's baton is stiff and hard, I want to mold it and polish it, to cure my fever once and for all, to bring its tasty honey to my lips, come, put your prick inside me, dig your spur into me, drill me with your tool, let's make love to each other as though possessed, the darkness is our mansion, put out the light that has guided me to you, the night, the solitude, the mice are enough for us, I'm chaste and modest, I don't want you to see me, your rod is tremendous, I'll take every last inch of it, I want it to exercise its prerogatives in the back of my throat, I'll take off my veil, my tulle headdress, my wig, my vocation requires discipline, the ability to relax and feel at ease, profound powers of concentration, an attribute such as yours is not for everyone, no novice could handle it, she'd fail instantly, she'd give up halfway through the test, she'd rake you with her incisors and canines, she'd gag, she'd puff and pant like a harpooned whale, false teeth get in the way and I can put mine in and take them out at will, store them away in their case, do my work without hindrance, with the kind assistance of the rodents' tiny tongues, vying with them for the privilege of tickling you and raising your tumulary rigor to its apotheosis, undertaking at last, blissful, confident, happy, overcome with emotion, in a fit of ecstasy, the illustrious deed, gradually causing your emblem to disappear from sight as if by magic, taking in the entire length of your incredible spear, that's the way, my love, don't move, don't pay any attention to the lights and the noise, it's no doubt beggars or sewer workers, come to hunt rats, to inspect the conduits, your good ten inches inside of me, it's as though my whole body were electrically charged, don't let your liqueur flow yet, hold it back a few seconds, I want to savor it, to be rejuvenated, to be like Dracula's beloved, or poor Doctor Frankenstein's, that movie we saw in Paris in a cheap, filthy neighborhood theater, remember, habibi?, we went downstairs and you locked yourself in the john with me, we made it together for five minutes the way we're doing right now while all the other women waited outside, heaving enormous sighs, frustrated, frantic, literally hollow-eyed with envy, I was exhausted but you insisted on beginning all over again, a real barbarian, you wouldn't lay down your arms, driven by an inexplicable urge even though the others were whispering outside the door, spying on us through a hole, shouting that the police were coming, and I felt terribly proud of the gift that was bestowed on me, I thanked heaven above, I begged Fate not to separate us, I remember that when you'd finished you wiped your sword clean by rubbing it on the wall, there wasn't any water or paper, you came out before I did, confronted the chorus of Parcae, and I thought I'd find you again once I got back to our seats, but you were nowhere to be seen, you'd sneaked out of the theater and left me in the lurch, it's no use trying to play dumb now because I know it was you, a weapon like yours isn't that easily

185

forgotten, it continues to hang in the panoply of one's memory, it retains its shamanistic powers through the years, your syrup is splendid, I bless the doctor who prescribed it, I down every last drop of it and lick the spoon, harking back to the days when there was rationing, your poor mousies are going to go hungry, do you realize that, you rascal?, you haven't lost your hard-on, it's still as stiff and persistent as before, I'm going to take off my clothes for it, for you, the Étincelle model from Pronuptia, the skirt with the ruffled train, the unconventional low-cut neckline, the rubber falsies, I want to ride it like a saddle, pump with my knees and elbows, there's no young chick more lithe and supple than I am, savoir faire can make up for one's lost youth if one has the will and the determination, no novice could compete with me, I'm a gold mine of know-how, an industrious spider with tentacles, my legs spread wide apart, just stay the way you are, never mind that they're staring at us, they're jealous of us, they're bored with the pap they get served at home, they'll never never know how sweet this molasses is, you've put it in me up to the hilt again, ach hada, d-dem?, I don't know what dem is, my love, but it's as though you'd deflowered me at my age, something's wrong with my insides these days, a touch of colitis perhaps, a little trickle of blood comes out sometimes, I'm

going to wipe it up with a Kleenex, I always keep a
packet of it handy, see there?, some came out, I'll
throw it away, no? you want me to give it to you? you
want to keep it? well, go ahead, it's all yours! an odd
whim if I may say so, ah I get it, you don't need to tell
me, I once went to a wedding way out in the desert,
it's as though we'd gotten married, you'll show it to
your family some day, the entire tribe will be overjoyed, they'll know I was a virgin when you took me

all of a sudden they turned on the floodlights
beams of glaring light projected from different angles, cameramen shouting and scurrying about, a
commentary delivered in an emphatic tone of voice
by a couple of reporters who advance toward you
with smiling faces, microphone in hand: ladies and
gentlemen, television viewers and radio listeners, Joe
Brown and Ben Hughes of the PB News team, or
words to that effect: as she abandons her kamasutric
position in terror, attempts to cover her violated
nakedness, oh heaven help me, my wig, my veil, the
Etincelle gown, the rubber falsies, my bridal headdress!: this exclusive broadcast by PB News, Journey
to the Center of the Earth, In the Bowels of Our City,
is pleased to present to you an extraordinary couple
who have sought happiness far from the hustle and

bustle of daily life, an original couple who have made their home, like hundreds and thousands of rodents, in the kingdom of perpetual night!: affixing the falsies so hurriedly that they slide around to her back, pointing strabismally outward, putting the wig on hind side to, pulling her panties up, frantically donning the polyester crêpe de Chine gown, grabbing up her leather handbag, forgetting in her haste to put her false teeth back in: the black doesn't move a muscle, imperturbably contemplates the frenetic activity round about him, seems to be floating in a state of down-cushioned drowsiness: his ace of spades maintains its rigidly erect position, his dusky hand is holding with singular delicacy what would appear to be a plain, ordinary Kleenex, and you scarcely blink an eye when the announcer exclaims my goodness and thrusts his toy in front of your face: how do you feel, sir?: a brief statement for our TV viewers and radio listeners?: but silence, silence, a vacant stare, a disturbing absence of ears, a throbbing, defiantly erect penis, and suddenly, wham, his jaws snap shut, his teeth bite down, he begins to devour the microphone voraciously, hey man, are you crazy?, consternation, commotion, screams, taking advantage of the confusion to flee, to disappear, to reel off like a moth blinded by the light, without the paschal candle, the headdress, shoes, false teeth, an old woman suddenly bowed down by the weight of years, hunchbacked because of the abnormal position of the tits, hey ma'am, miss, don't go away, our TV viewers and radio listeners are waiting for you, a few simple words of greeting, the city has its eyes fixed on you, don't disappoint the audience that is watching you and admiring you, it's your chance to let them get to know you, think of the millions of spectators, be nice to them, smile, give them at least a smile

HYPOTHESES CONCERNING
A DWELLER IN HELL

EVERYBODY TO THE CATHEDRAL
OF LEARNING!
let us take advantage of this opportunity offered us to
question Science!
let us hasten to drink of the waters of human
wisdom!
let us gather together in the basilican shadow offered
us by its selfless maternal vocation!
researchers
sociologists
executives

students
mere curious onlookers
excited mothers!
with the acute, tingling sensation, the impatient expectation of a person about to attend the première of a super-spectacular show, hastily making up your face, touching up your dark half-moon of mascara, assuring yourself of the sanguine perfection of your new tube of lipstick
hurry up, darling, we'll be late, there's going to be an overflow crowd, everybody will be there, there won't be nearly enough seats, it's the big event of the day!
and from bus stops, taxi stands, especially chartered excursion buses, endlessly long cars with the silent, fluvial, menacing look of crocodiles, the eager multitude flocks to the monumental building, bunches up at its side entrances, mounts the stairways, makes its way inside, roams about beneath the neo-Gothic vaulted ceilings, fights for the last vacant seats in the hall on whose platform, taking advantage of the momentary absence of the academic authorities, reporters, photographers, fans, students from the school of journalism riddle the corpus delicti with exploding flashbulbs and questions
ghost, specter, monster come from the nether world? a disturbing intrusion in any event: an oneiric apparition: a sudden, insolent challenge

191

absorbed in the obverse side of the spectacle he is creating: dusky bare feet, insensitive to the rigors of the season: ragged, threadbare pants with improvised skylights at the knees: a scarecrow's overcoat with collar raised to conceal a double absence

as the telephone switchboard of the alma mater finds itself swamped with local and long-distance calls, requests for information, offers of contracts, proposals for a stage tour, a photo-exclusive for filmed commercials, a pocket edition of Memoirs with fabulous press runs

private interviews as well, pleas for autographs, photographs with a personal dedication, exchanges of correspondence, offers of friendship, possible marriage

I am five feet three inches tall, weigh two hundred five pounds, have blue eyes and blonde hair, am a practicing Catholic, of Lithuanian descent, a Pisces, unmarried, no children, extremely interested in your career, personal tastes, plans for the future, leisure-time activities, experiences, would like to receive a photo of you and would send one of myself in return

unanswered questions, conjectures, comments exchanged in a half-whisper by the crowd in the jam-packed auditorium, beginning to show signs of impatience as it awaits the panel of scholars and spe-

cialists, their official opinion, their decision, their
conclusion handed down as though it were immutable law, a just sentence admitting of no appeal
where is this creature from?
what language does it speak?
how did it get here?
how long has it been living in the catacombs?
why has it chosen to cohabit with rats?
booing and catcalling, whistling, and finally breaking
into applause because the long-awaited egghead experts have at last made their appearance: with the
grave, solemn, serious countenances and demeanor of
judges, they have mounted the platform and taken
their assigned places around the semicircular table, to
the right of the armchair in which the phenomenal
subject of their inquiry is sitting with a blank expression on his face, absorbed in the contemplation of
a wrinkled piece of Kleenex, making incoherent gestures, waving his fist at the audience in a vaguely
threatening gesture
a silence falls, they are about to begin their discussion, the chairman shakes his little bell, extracts a
number of sheets of paper from the pocket of his suit
coat, clears his throat before speaking into the microphone, drinks a sip of water, announces the opening
of the debate, briefly introduces each of his col-

leagues, sits down, I've had my say and now I turn the floor over to you

ethnologically speaking, this case is quite simple and straightforward, the subject is a member of the Lingha tribe, whose original home was the Niger and which today is scattered throughout various States of the South Sahara region, his cranium, the conformation of his bones, the length and strength of his extremities correspond exactly with those of this most unusual ethnic group to which I devoted my doctoral dissertation, half a dozen books translated into a number of languages, a documentary film sponsored by the National School of Anthropology, and hundreds of articles and studies published in various specialized periodicals, my first intuition, on viewing the PB News program, was confirmed by the fact that the subject's ears were missing, which is to say, he had cut them off in accordance with a very common practice among his people, a few shots from my feature-length film, taken during a sacred initiation ceremony, are sufficient to prove that this type of mutilation is an extremely frequent practice, note for example that the group of dancers, the leader, his assistants, the medicine man standing on the left, the one wearing the necklace of seeds, all have bobbed noses, this being a sign of nobility, self-amputations take place in public, under the influence of drugs, and even young children witness this spectacle, here is the footage I filmed of one of these rites, I advise sensitive souls not to look, the candidate, note his bulging eyes, his contorted face, his mouth flecked with foam, is brandishing the knife with which he is about to lop off, watch closely, his right ear, whop, that's it, in a single stroke, with no anesthesia whatsoever, an act that would appear to be painless since, as you can see with your own eyes, even though he's dripping blood, he continues to dance about wildly, it is my belief that these images are incontrovertible evidence that should convince even the most skeptical viewer, but as further proof I shall point out that the males of this ethnic group are typified, as is the case of their fellow who is here before you, by the gigantic, truly inordinate dimensions of their sex organ!

voices: how did he happen to come to our city? can you communicate with him in his own language?

no, I humbly confess to you that I was unable to do so, this particular individual expresses himself solely by means of onomatopoeias and grunts, he has been separated from his kinfolk for reasons that I have no knowledge of and I am unable to shed any light on them inasmuch as they lie beyond the research frame-work of science, but the most likely hypothesis is that he has forgotten his language in the course of the many long years that he has lived in isolation, without any sort of human contact, in a dark, secluded world

I for my part am of the opinion, though I in no way claim that my theory contradicts the brilliant conclusions of my colleague, that the question of his presence among us, beneath the asphalt of the city in which we live, is absolutely fundamental, since once we reject the improbable hypothesis that a branch of his tribe emigrated to our continent (how? when? by what means?) or that the subject in question swam across the Atlantic (laughter from the audience), we are obliged to resort to the deductive method, that is to say, to take the very few facts that we have at our disposal as our point of departure and work back from there to the essential problems that present themselves, thereby resolving the mystery that his inexplicable presence gives rise to

I beg your pardon, but I am of the belief that the inductive leap would be more enlightening!

it may well be valid within your sphere of competence, namely linguistics, but certainly not in the field of sociology!

a voice: isn't it possible that the application of the probability calculus would prove useful?

yes, on condition, of course, that the factors that we

are dealing with are verifiable, this being the same obstacle that we encounter with computers, the work they do will be perfect if and when the facts and figures fed into them are absolutely valid, in other words, the operations they perform may at one and the same time be impeccable and erroneous, insofar as they are based on unreliable data

it seems to me that we are drifting away from the main subject of this debate, which is, or ought to be, as I see it, the individual himself, since despite the fact that the enigma of his origins, the obscure circumstances whereby he arrived in our sewers understandably intrigue the audience gathered together here, such questions, in addition to being extremely difficult to resolve, strike me as being relatively secondary as far as the subject's archetypical behavior is concerned, and hence this is tantamount to straying from the real question at hand, which is to decipher the profound meaning of the one certain fact we possess concerning him, that is to say his decision to live in the catacombs, all by himself, lulled by the dull rumbling sounds of the bowels of the city which, like those of the human being, reject inassimilable products by expelling them through conduits and connecting pipes into the anal cloaca where he was discovered, this is the key factor in his case history, and since there is no point in overwhelming you with otiose scholarly quotations or theories, I shall merely draw your attention to the symbolic import of his behavior, fleeing, firstly, the world in order to take shelter in the cozy, kindly, nourishing intimacy of the womb, rejecting, secondly, the alienating image of himself that his fellow man sends back to him like a hateful glass in which he sees himself reflected, overcoming the infantile trauma of the mirror thanks to the darkness, and reeducating, finally, his sense of hearing, after having rid himself, both literally and symbolically, of his ears sensitive to the noise, the agitation, the hostile intrusions of the outside world, habituating it to the quiet, soothing, muffled echoes of the uterine phase, nostalgically returning, to sum up and conclude my remarks, to his existence as a fetus!

voice: your interpretation is tempting, but it is not based on verifiable facts, and psychoanalytic treatment would be required to shed light on these limit-conditions!

I am entirely in agreement with the observation that we have just heard, since the very beginning of this discussion all we have been offered is suppositions, indemonstrable conjectures, hasty and frequently gratuitous theories, and therefore, in order to skirt such pitfalls and avoid the vagueness and confusion that this sort of symposium often suffers from, I propose that from now on we abandon mere assumptions and symbols in favor of an approach that is no doubt dull and pedestrian and unexciting, but at the same time more suitable to the strictly scientific aim of clarification that is our guiding principle

my esteemed colleague will pardon me if I remind him that at the very heart of scientific endeavor, of each one of its advances and discoveries, the creative vision, the powers of imagination of men of genius have always played a primordial role!

naturally, and I am sorry if I expressed myself badly or if what I said was misunderstood, I merely wanted to suggest that, in order to compensate for the lack of solid data on which to base a reconstruction of the past of this individual and draw tentative conclusions as to his language, we adopt a more modest methodological approach and content ourselves with what we have, his clothing, movements, gestures, facial expressions, grunts, that is to say, practice a rigorous semiological reading of these elements, and while making no concession whatsoever to diachrony, try to extrapolate little by little the communications code, the subjacent signifying structure

my good friend appears to conceive of synchronic and diachronic factors as totally and irreducibly excluding each other, despite the fact that in those very same scholarly circles that he so greatly admires and from whose sources he so eagerly drinks, even though he frequently forgets to cite them, a theory is beginning to be developed which holds that their dynamics in fact manifest themselves in terms of complementarity and convergence!

I am quite aware of that, but as you yourself concede, this is still mere theory, a working hypothesis whose adequacy remains to be demonstrated

voice: isn't it possible that information theory might have something to contribute to the subject that you are discussing?

yes, certainly, it's my specialty in fact, and I am naturally surprised that none of my honorable colleagues present here has made the slightest reference to it thus far, the quantity of information contained in a given unit of communication is inversely proportional, as all of you are aware, to its index of probability, that is to say, the greater its degree of improbability, the greater the wealth of information it will convey, hence one can easily deduce that the appearance of an individual marked by the striking peculiarities and within the singular circumstances characterizing the object of this symposium constitutes an event of transcendent importance from the point of view of information theory, and in order to give you a clearer idea of the contribution that it has to offer with regard to the subject at hand, I shall take the liberty of reading you a brief monograph, prefaced by a kind and somewhat flattering introduction by my revered teacher at the University of (his words are drowned out at this point by furious protests from the audience)

voices: stop blowing your own horn!, you're a bunch of publicity hounds!, this discussion isn't leading anywhere!, stop touting your theories, all of you, and tell us about the troglodyte!

the chairman: quiet, please, if all of you try to talk at once nobody will hear a word!

I should like to conclude my remarks by briefly mentioning the brilliant theses of

shouts: no, no!

very well then, I shall say no more, if you down there in the audience are going to confuse freedom of inquiry with tumult and shouting, you can jolly well try to go on with this symposium all by yourselves!

I regret that I must disagree with my distinguished colleague in public, but I find myself obliged to remind him that formal freedom can and inevitably will turn into boos and catcalls whenever an audience tumbles to the fact that the wool is being pulled over their eyes, that the real, urgent, and dramatic problem that has brought them to this public forum is being used as a mere pretext for a byzantine debate by half a dozen mandarins who have taken refuge in the ivory tower of their academic privileges, completely withdrawn from and insensitive to the profound aspirations and needs of the masses, specialists possessed of an Olympian disdain for anything and everything that does not concern the minute field of their specialty, totally absorbed in the pointless task of decorating the interior walls of a boat that has sprung leaks everywhere and is irrevocably doomed to sink!

voices: bravo, hear hear, well put!

the subject under discussion at this symposium, and please excuse my brutal frankness, is purely and simply the question of the flagrant injustice of the socioeconomic system in which we live, its merciless use of the mechanisms of oppression that it has at its disposal to destroy the human being and make a miserable wretch of him, its concerted plundering of the riches and resources of this earth, its rapacious appropriation of the surplus value created by the worker and the salaried employee, its elitist conception of culture aimed at denying the people access to educational facilities and deliberately keeping it in ignorance, the brutish, inhuman state into which it plunges the individual, forcing him, as is the case with the unfortunate creature you see before you, to keep his distance from society and the toils of an infamous system of production, to turn his back on its egregious lies and criminal propaganda, to seek refuge in a less cruel and repressive prehistory, inasmuch as, obliged to rely entirely on his own devices, he has not been able, by his own efforts alone, to arrive at a clear awareness of his situation, to forge an intellectual weapon enabling him to defend himself against the alienation of which he is a victim and glimpse the ray of hope of a new society with neither exploiters nor exploited which, with the brightness of noon, is beginning to filter into, to illuminate our decrepit and dilapidated edifice! (numerous murmurs of disapproval)

voice: stick to the subject and spare us the fancy speeches!

the protests of the lackeys of the system will not still my voice, my proud reference to that radiant beacon that is the only hope of salvation for mankind, that risks being clawed to death by the great wild beast in its last throes, brandishing as its supreme weapon of intimidation the blackmailing threat of nuclear war, the prospect of a terrible cataclysm!

voices: that's enough of that!, shut your trap!, we know your spiel by heart!

well, you're going to have to put up with it once more, because there is no one who can halt the march of history and in the Popular Republic of (his words are drowned out in the uproar) a spectacle such as the miserable wretch that we are now contemplating would be absolutely inconceivable, in that country exploitation has been forever abolished, the proletariat has come to power, there is equal opportunity for all, the people control education and have taken the last redoubts of the moribund culture of the preceding regime by assault!

voices: button your lip!

in that country (the outcry from the audience interrupts him once again) the masses have taken their destiny in their own hands and instead of vegetating in the physical and intellectual indolence that is the rule here, they avidly read the classics of our doctrine, steep themselves in the collective study of the Works of that tremendous Leader whose incredible popularity is revealed by the fact that his words and his thoughts are continually cited in discussions, meetings, speeches, private conversations, by the countless number of photographs of him lovingly displayed in the home of each and every citizen, by the spontaneity and fervor with which grateful youngsters endeavor to surpass each other in the making of drawings and the composing of poems in his honor, conscious of his gigantic contribution to the progress of mankind, the development of human personality, the imperishable legacy of our species!

various members of the panel: this is inadmissible!

stentorian voice: go live in your Republic if you like
it so much!
shouts and cries: that's right, that's right, let him
clear out of here this minute!!
the chairman: gentlemen, calm down!

but no one is listening to him: the members of the
audience express their displeasure by pounding furiously on their desks: a number of them rise to their
feet, climb up on their seats, point an accusing index
finger at the panelists: the experts on the platform
argue with each other, attempt to pick up the thread
of previous speeches, invoke the rigor and exactitude
of science, shield themselves behind the untouchable
figure of some sacred cow of their discipline, aggressively cite his pronouncements as though hurling
thunderbolts, inveigh against each other, accuse each
other of being sectarians, shallow thinkers, dismal
failures: when the group of travelers from Sahara
Tours unobtrusively enters the auditorium the din is
deafening: the guide tries to translate for them the
explanations provided in the publicity folder put out
by the Tourist Office, but finds himself obliged
to give up his efforts to orient them, despite the fact
that they are equipped with modern, noise-filtering,

ultrasensitive earphones: frightened, confused, they huddle around him without letting go for an instant, because of the swarm of pickpockets and the general lack of security in native hotels, of the bundles and parcels in which their miscellaneous goods and chattels are neatly wrapped: little metal boxes full of their immovables, worn packs of cards, anatomical plates in color, treatises on the art of love and aphrodisiac recipes, Korans, magic formulas, ancient prayer books

they are all here

the simpleminded soul stroking the strings of his rebec, lovinglycradling it like a wet nurse

the veiled woman who tells fortunes

the miracle-monger bending down to draw graffiti with his bit of chalk

the young acrobat dressed in a little short jacket and bright-colored balloon pants

the Gnaua dancers, in immaculate trousers and blouses, smooth, dark legs, unadorned and quintessentially naked

the giant with the strong skull shaved perfectly bare, the thick stubby neck, broad shoulders, coppery skin, thick lips, the Mongol mustache trickling down past his chin, the gold-capped teeth

the elderly mime decked out in a blond wig

the two clowns wearing donkey's ears and rudimentary disguises
the sinewy flute players, with swarthy complexions
and bushy mustaches, accompanied by the transvestite in a filmy veil, female garments, an embroidered
sash
the collector of lizards, as hieratic as a billy goat
the public scribe with a pen, an inkwell, and a
wrinkled sheet of parchment
the tradesmen
the expounders of the Law of Islam
the craftsmen
the shopboys
the students of the Koran
visibly ignorant of the meaning of the spectacle that
they are contemplating, the hubbub of intermingled
speeches and shouts, the two opposing platforms, the
violent confrontation of the panelists towering over
them, until finally one of the tour group spies a silent
presence in the shadow, crouching fiercely in its seat,
still lost in hermetic contemplation of a rumpled
Kleenex
without quite believing what might turn out to be
yet another illusion of the senses, he cautiously points
the figure out to his neighbors, holds a consultation
with them, transmits the message in a whisper

look there, don't you recognize him?
who?
the one sitting on the chair
where?
up there, next to the speakers' table
tbarak-allah, I see him now!
and so on: yes, you're right, he's from Marrakesh, I
know him by sight, he used to work years ago in the
tannery, who could possibly have brought him to
such a strange, faraway place?
unable to contain themselves, at once delighted and
bewildered, they motion to him to try to attract his
attention, invite him to come join them, hey, fellah,
don't you even remember your countrymen?
the giant with the shaved skull puts his fingers to his
mouth and gives a piercing whistle that wreaks the
sudden miracle of silencing the uproar: all eyes focus
on him, and even the cave dweller appears to rouse
himself from his morose drowsiness: still in a half-
stupor he looks at the jubilant group of tourists and
little by little his tense features relax, his eyes begin to
shine and move again, his thick, rigid lips that look as
though they were made of cardboard slowly curve
into an incredulous smile
he suddenly gets up from his seat, leaves the platform,
scales the flight of steps leading to the amphitheater
in a few swift strides, falls into the arms of the first

compatriot who greets him, plants a quadruple kiss of peace on his rough cheeks, scarcely able to contain his tears of ecstatic joy

the ahlan-wa-sahlan, fain kunti?, ach had el ghiba?, marhaba bik, s-salamu ali-kums echo melodiously in the auditorium

panelists and spectators witness this exultant family reunion in open-mouthed astonishment, and when the object of the debate disappears with the intruders, the chairman sadly announces that the symposium has come to a close

LIKE WIND IN A NET

full of holes: the wind blows in all directions, there is
no way of taking cover: totally abandoned: an orphan
plain, shifting sand, wretchedness, hostility, helplessness, whirlwinds of dust, obsessive rage, rancor: not
even believing his eyes: an invitation to weigh an-
chor, escape, arrive safely in port: a deceptive promise,
a surrender endlessly postponed: an interminable succession of dunes, unlimited space, horizontal death:
udders, rotundities, verdure, illusory abundance: a
sign presaging happiness but bringing perdition;
straining against the wind, putting down roots in the

harsh ground, resisting the inhospitable environment, feeding on air like stubborn scrub brush: in rags and tatters, barefoot, penned in with the filthy flock, wandering about like a sleepwalker, knowing nothing of the world beyond the ravenous landscape: only the scantiest information about himself and others: fragments of phrases, sudden, prolonged silences, looks of scorn or pity: knowing that you are a bastard without yet understanding what that means: invisibility, people acting as if he didn't exist, he's ugly-looking, nobody caresses me affectionately, his mother weaned him immediately, he grew up a wild child, everybody laughs at your ears: taking the flock to graze in dry gullies, bundling himself up in his blanket, a crude caparison: sheltered from the sun and the cold, from the yellow powder of the dust storms: there is nothing behind what your eye encompasses: solar cycles, redundancy, monotony, words and gestures repeated to the point of satiety: trying nanny goats' teats on the sly, sucking warm milk, imagining another universe, gracious and welcoming: discovering one day that your mother is sick and secretly hoping for her death: master at last of my own wretchedness, making your escape from the corpse with a deerlike bound: walking, walking on and on, without ever once turning your head, new tribes, new pastures, seeking shelter with the flocks, begging, scrounging for food: he lives on his own, let's tell him he can bed down with the cattle, eat with us, tend the sheep: nighttime conversations round the warm fire at the end of each day: hearing the others talk about me as though I weren't there: nobody looks after him, his mother's dead, he's simpleminded, he answers in grunts, and inevitably, remarks about my ears: and the longing to flee, like bait placed before you: almost the moment someone takes you in you run away: feral, untamed, a nomad, drifting aimlessly, impossible to keep him: marauding, making the dogs bark, the object of cruel jokes, the victim of hails of stones: listening: he looks like a monster: listening: even the devil would refuse to take him to hell with him: but going on, paying no attention, receiving from time to time the solace of alms, a bowl of milk, a charitable hand, a tender smile: making his way out of the naked desert: approaching a town for the first time in his life and admiring the impeccable symmetry of the stars: constellations traced with a ruling pen that increase in size as you draw closer: miraculously encapsulated bubbles: electric lights: standing there in stupefaction for a long time, feeling an immediate rush of happiness, forgetting everything he has left behind: the past, ashes, dreams: the image of your own ugliness: an ungainly body, clumsy extremities,

212

a pockmarked face: banding together with other youngsters, becoming a marketplace rat, shining shoes, running errands, keeping out of reach of the law, sleeping in the open in the night air: being initiated into the arcana of their nocturnal games: hearing them steal away from their straw sleeping mats to go off with militiamen or soldiers, lunar pimping, sly complicity, the secrecy of shadows, the conniving darkness of the cemetery: spying on their caresses, whispers, penetrations, panting breaths: a harmonious, crude coupling of bodies that attests to the bitter isolation of yours: nobody wants me: a shaved head, donkey's ears, piss like a mule's, an enormous dong: walking on, clothed in rags and covered with grime, confronting others' stares with callous indifference, with no need for a mirror's harsh accusation to tell you that their verdict will go against you: hastening to the halca, filling my head with stories, admiring the silver-tongued halaiquí, his gleaming smile, his talents as a buffoon, a moralist, a poet: exhibitions of strength and skill, an incomparable gift for words, recitations from the Koran: laughing till you cry at his risqué tales, his sudden onomatopoeic outbursts, his obscene gestures: young, self-assured, clad in a superb djellabah, there's nobody like him, he needs only to stand there, invoke the blessing of heaven, fold his arms in thoughtful concentration,

213

use the charisma of the spoken word to magnetize young and old, capture their attention, keep them absolutely quiet, fascinated, enthralled, dwellers in a world that is pure and perfect, as luminously clear as an algebraic proof: identifying yourself totally with him, proud of your learning and your eloquence, the offensive ease with which you accumulate coins and prodigally spend them on intoxicating love-trysts or the mild euphoria of kif: greetings, hand-kissing, salaams, smiles: all the girls are looking at me: affection, gentleness, the lingering odor of the harem: traveling as he does from town to town, reciting the Koran from memory, bending wills with the warm intonations of your voice: divining hidden beauties beneath the chaste modesty of veils, arranging secret meetings with a mere wink of the eye, cold nights burning hot with passion, delicious excesses, shared intoxication, fervent ejaculations: vows forgotten at the break of dawn, divine fulfillment become mere mortal tedium, making your escape with a light heart, surfeit, aloofness, a thief's furtive footsteps: more fairs, shrine festivals, markets, new conquests, further disillusionment, faithful only to yourself, a perpetual trickster: an unbridled imagination, danger, wrath, he's turning against me, attacking tooth and nail: sloth, sleep, hash, model airplane glue, whatever: getting stoned out of my mind at the age of ten, my fate

214

is sealed, if people give him a helping hand it's worse: knowing beyond the shadow of a doubt that there's no way out: an inescapable destiny, retreating inward, poverty fear walls closing in nothingness ugliness: growing nonetheless, feeling the heavy weight of your member between your legs, he's hung like a stud ass, come on, show it to us, let us see it, pull your pants legs up farther so we can have a look at it, no woman is going to want to take it, you're going to have to make it with a mare: bloody jokes, ear-pulling, animal resignation: the halaiquí has gone off, the fiesta's over, they've taken the tents down, he may not come back: lighting out, abandoning the dirty little village, following the caravan of itinerant fairgrounds merchants and entertainers, living on a few handfuls of nuts, loitering about other marketplaces, military barracks in desolate desert areas: hanging around the garrisons of Legionnaires and Spahis, doing little odd jobs for the soldiers, washing out mess kits, wolfing down the leftovers, picking up garbage: a practiced parasite, an expert at collecting slops, a master at gathering bones: a sick world, infested with alien objects, nothing for me, everything for them, creeping corruption, the simulacrum of a life: dust, sand, simoons, completely silted up inside, no use trying to keep clean, your soul is filthy: subsisting, vegetating, wandering from one regiment to another, a bird of prey hovering about waiting for carrion, with the bald head, the stench, the insatiable appetite of a vulture: dawn, the portent of new calamities, a Pandora's box, an illusory light: but bringing surprises too now and then, unexpected breaks in routine: watching a military parade file past eminent dignitaries: feverish preparations for a celebration: guttural orders, a great to-do, a general policing, spitting and polishing: an outdoor show with a star from the metropolis: canvas-covered quartermasters' carts, improvised dressing rooms: sentries posted at the doors, soldiers making a nuisance of themselves, curious peeks through the curtains, red hair, bursts of laughter, hips swaying provocatively: a wooden stage, a simple decor, ropes of tinsel, draperies, spotlights, an eager audience, men from the barracks squatting on their heels, applause, catcalls: a brass band playing patriotic airs, a nasal accordion, homesickness, tightrope walking, magic tricks, folk groups: one-act farces, the obligatory curtain-raisers before the long-anticipated appearance of the artiste: the highlight of the evening: an enigmatic, sibylline figure lurking backstage, waiting to make a sensational entrance: feathers, sequins, satin slippers, a sexiloquent dance: enthusiastic cheers from the audience, cries of encore, encore, waves of applause, flowers, a diva's deep curtsies: sinuous hands, prom-

issory curves, suggestive writhings, slow pubic oscillation: contemplating in fascination the point of convergence: a forbidden paradise, a black triangle, a garden of delights: knowing that it isn't for me yet still wanting it badly, watching the quartermaster's cart in which she is lodged, spying on her in the pandering celestine starlight, seeing her slip out amid the shadows with swift, stealthy footsteps: furtive silhouettes, Spahis on maneuvers, muffled footfalls, the softness of the cemetery: hugging the ground, witnessing the successive couplings: moans, electric currents, inductions, panting followed by sudden opaque silence: the time necessary to stand up, step aside so a buddy can take his turn, produce his voltaic flux, disconnect again: waiting until the last husky brute comes in her, scrubs his rough bayonet with sand, disappears like the others, vanishes amid the tombs: there are just the two of you now, she continues to lie there, you listen to her breathing, little by little recovering her strength
merde, j'ai les reins brisés!
breaking the spell, drawing closer to her, forcing your shaky legs onward, finally getting a good look at her: leaning over her nurse's kit, indiscreetly inventorying her miscellaneous treasures: lipsticks, face creams, eyeliner, vials of perfume, foundation makeup: balls of cotton, an ostentatious jar of vaseline, mint-

scented paper handkerchiefs, a package of sanitary napkins: frontal hemispheres hinting at tumescence, provocative, erectile nipples, a deep, disturbingly available hollow below her belly: the greedy fullness of her lips shows through her veil, her eyes drill into you like point-blank pistol shots: eyelashes loaded with mascara, a simple beauty mark on her cheekbone, a stirring, throaty voice, a romantic interpretation of Morocco

eh, toi, le gamin, qu'est-ce que c'est que ce bâton qui te pend entre tes jambes?

no derision in her voice, no scorn: merely curiosity, friendliness, affection, let me come closer, her fingers explore the rigor mortis, she gives an incredulous smile

ce n'est pas vrai! mais c'est énorme!

a wink of complicity, a swift thrust of her tongue, cries of astonishment, prolonged fervor, sincere admiration: delicate, expert hands palpate the reality of the miracle, grope, measure, test the weight of it as they fondle it: increasing wonder, amazement, stupefaction as she rummages inside her nurse's kit, fishes out a tape measure, extends it from the base to the tip, tenderly encircles the diameter, gives a start, rejoices, pretends to grimace in terror

you don't say a word, enthralled, ecstatic, unable to assimilate such happiness, you don't stink, you're not filthy, his ears are missing, the woman rises to her feet, sighs, kisses you, says she'll be back, the two of you will make love, we'll fuck, remote catacombs, distant cemeteries, she'll never forget what I look like, she'll recognize you by the length of your rod, keep it for me, take good care of it, I'll come back for it sooner or later, she'll make it hers, it will fill the hollow of her cave, I'll take it in, I swear to you, down to the very bottom of my throat

NEWS FROM THE BEYOND

they were waiting for her around the corner, or to be more precise, right at the entrance to the sewer: the train of the bedraggled Pronuptia wedding dress in polyester crêpe de Chine trailing along after her: the headdress, the veil, the wig, the high-heeled shoes, the false teeth lost: battered and tattered, ragged and ruined, as the old song goes

a team of five or six, equipped with everything necessary to fulfill the mission that they had been sent on, as you found out later, for reasons of dignity and prestige: obeying harsh orders impassively handed

220

down from the very top ranks: you had been briefly interrogated, taken into custody, drugged, smuggled across the border by other messengers disguised as executives or tourists, thanks to the diplomatic pouch

when I woke up, I was in paradise once again

the first consequence: recovering your eternal status, taking on once more the attributes of a candid, pink-cheeked, perennial youth: a soft, smooth face, perfect features, a cheerful expression, a limpid gaze, an imperturbable smile: a cascade of blond hair, always impeccably coiffed without the need of permanents or shampoos, worn cropped to waist length as regulations required: a slender, delicate, agile, svelte body, deformed neither by fatty posterior convexities nor by an anterior bipolar, tumescent, spheroidal bust: free also of those superfluous apertures which, to their misfortune, afflict the ordinary run of base mortals: bright celestial eyes eternally delighting in the beatific contemplation of some ethereal, diaphanous scene, graceful attitudes and gestures, swift, winged movements, radiant wisdom and beauty: a voice whose timbre is soft, harmonious, exquisite, ideal for chanting deogratias and antiphonies, praising the Lord, the Intercessoress, and members of the executive, perpetually hymning the benefits of the sublime system that we enjoy

the great challenge that lies before us: how to perfect what is already perfect, how to better the conditions of an order that is manifestly unbetterable?: a problem that puts our constant dedication to real progress in life to the test and is the object of continual, fruitful discussions at Summit meetings and within the small circle of friends who watch over Mother's health: periodically setting new, more ambitious goals, transmitting directives through hierarchical channels, seeing to it that they are properly carried out by inferior choirs: fostering in the latter a wholesome spirit of emulation and voluntary personal service: bringing the precepts and maxims of the Guide and Mediatrix to the most remote corners, endeavoring to ensure that they are read and reread until they have been committed to memory, keeping our ears open to make certain no error of diction liable to adulterate the correct interpretation of the text creeps in, assuring the obedience and fidelity of the intermediate cadres, deciding with them the date when the objectives will be triumphantly achieved: billions of Paternosters, trillions of Avemarias, tirelessly repeated prayers to save the blessed souls atoning for their sins or fleeing the beastly temptations that lie in wait for the hapless rational being: properly publicizing the example of one or another especially self-abnegating guardian who has spontaneously tripled the number of honors awarded those of his particular choir and station: disseminating the heartfelt words of thanks and congratulation of the charismatic head of the Secretariat: unceasing quantitative progress that breaks all previous records, incredible as they were, without thereby neglecting what we might call the aesthetic aspect, our more and more demanding standards of taste and quality: subtly hieratic attitudes and gestures, faultless modulation of our voices as we chant our prayers, demonstrating exemplary joy and enthusiasm in our general assemblies and at official ceremonies, expanding the serenity and fixity of our smiles to the very limits of ineffability

our most effective and dependable method: persuasion: convincing one who has wandered or strayed from the straight and narrow path traced in the Book of the dire consequences of his errant ways, both for himself and the community: exhorting him not to imitate the example of Medea, whose conduct Ovid severely censured when he put in her mouth that telling phrase *video meliora proboque, deteriora se-*

quor that betrays her weakness, her instability, her resignation: leading him, gently but firmly, to scrupulously examine his conscience, to search his soul, to have confidence in the therapeutic value of a pitiless, truly sincere, exhaustive, faithful self-criticism: is it not undeniable that the laws of history, our everyday sense-experiences prove, beyond all reasonable doubt, that our system is the most just and most suitable one, inasmuch as it does away with all possible contradictions or differences between the individual and the collectivity?: is not rebelling against the latter tantamount to taking up arms against one's own self?: since the good of both is blended in a single perfect chord, to whom would the bizarre idea of fighting to destroy himself ever occur save to a wretched, shame-ridden suicide, resolved to end his days in order not to be obliged to live the joyous, blissful life of his fellows?: if we were hard-hearted and insensitive, as our detractors maintain, we would allow the misguided messenger, deserter, turncoat, to plunge all by himself into the abysses where he would inevitably doom himself to perdition: but our sense of brotherhood and duty, the luminous examples of the Leader, the Mediatrix, and the members of the executive inspire us not to abandon our fallen comrade in his sterile delirium, his sad and ridiculous false pride: our solicitude toward you is the fruit of a deep-

seated, well-founded conviction: only a schizo-
phrenic, a clinical case could lower himself and
behave as you have: we will help you, patiently,
lovingly, to recover from your rebellious and insid-
ious illness

you have given rise to a great deal of gossip, and you
know it: as was inevitable, your case came up in conversations and you were, so to speak, the talk of the
town: when the glorious Intercessoress learned of
your escapades and the extremes of degradation into
which you had fallen, she remained in seclusion in
her apartments for several days, stricken, according to
rumors that filtered down from her secretariat, with a
severe, stubborn, splitting headache: if you had a single ounce of gratitude left in the bottom of your
heart you would hasten to prostrate yourself before
Her and beseech Her pardon for your indecent and
disorderly conduct: is this any way to repay her for
the innumerable benefits and favors that she has be-
nevolently, generously, lavished upon you?: a humble personal letter of contrition and firm promises to
mend your ways would help to salve her wounds, to
soothe her grieving Mother's heart with a discreet
and fragrant balm: do it for your sake, for our
sake, for Her sake: search within yourself, draw

strength from your noblest and purest sentiments, write out a list of your errors: deviationism, violation of statutes, reformist hallucinations, bourgeois vices, abandonment of the correct line as laid down in official directives, perversions and bizarre inclinations characteristic of historical stages that have been transcended: allow yourself to be inspired by the example of the rest of us as well: the contagious fervor with which we meet the norms, exceed the goals that have been set, plan glorious moments such as the one we are living just now: thus enabling yourself to escape from the inferno in which you find yourself buried, to abjure your errors of the past, to take a clear and forthright position consistent with our paradigmatic social philosophy: you need only draw up a detailed account of everything you have said and done during your ill-fated forays into the world: don't forget: upholding the brilliant future of our exemplary type of society will be the best way of ensuring that your own future will be a brilliant one

always the same mumbo-jumbo, blackmail, propaganda, sermonizing: having to listen to the same old song and dance day and night: abnormality, subjectivism, involution, regressive, orgiastic tendencies: the headaches that, perverted creature that I am, I inflicted on the Mediatrix (caused, rather, in your opinion, by the weight of the diadems and jewels with which she extravagantly adorns herself), the inflammatory image of choirs absorbed in hymning the praises or chanting the liturgy hailing our supreme, co-opted board of directors (a scene she found unbearable: repetitive, burdensome, monotonous, stultifying)

their stubborn insistence that you write your life's story, reexamine your every act and thought, feed their morbid curiosity by recounting a thousand piquant episodes: the way I met you, when and how we made love together, the exact size of your tool: they wanted to know everything, absolutely everything, down to the very last detail: did you kiss well?, did you bite my breasts?, what did your serum taste like?, what did your scimitar look like?: swooning with jealousy, consumed with envy of our ephemeral glory, despite the impassive, severe attitude they invariably adopted in the course of the confrontations and interrogations to which they subjected you: as though one's senses had a memory!: as though love were not purely and simply a beautiful, impermanent collection of fleeting moments!: useless to try to get across to them that I didn't even know who you were: that you had no idea or had forgotten what his name was and what he looked like: that my love was ever and

227

always the same and your body, appearance, bearing, attributes kept changing imperceptibly: she had no postcards showing them in the act, nobody had filmed them fucking, your life had flowed past like a vague, chance dream: but they kept after me, determined to wrest a confession from me, to savor with gloating, gluttonous pleasure unheard-of salacious details: positively drooling, I swear, the moment the comrades in charge of the proceedings turned their backs: come on, tell us, what was that beggar in the sewers like?: is it true he had a picador's lance thirteen inches long?: how hard was it and what was its diameter?: did you take every last bit of it?: how the devil did you manage to get it down your throat?: their delicately pink, purely ornamental mouths quivered with impatience and fury as they imagined the heroic feat that my meritorious fellatio represented: their depressingly flat chests, their plain, rudimentary busts, lacking the indispensable curves and clefts, burned, palpitated, shivered, victims of an unknown emotion, whose inevitable frustration took the form, as is quite understandable, of fits of rage and indignation: filthy pig, swine, aren't you disgusted with yourself and covered with shame at having fallen so low?: they ranted and raved, played doctor-and-nurse, lifted up my hideous linen tunic and jubilantly assured themselves of my anatomical hermeticism (a celluloid

228

kewpie doll, that's what I really was!) and they, hypo-
crites that they were, stripped naked too, presented
the ignominious spectacle of bodies like ironing
boards, performed a simulacrum of coitus, using the
flute on which one of them (the most sanctimonious
of all) accompanied the sempiternal hymns of praise
to the Guide and the head everlasting of the Secretariat: come on, spill the beans, out with it!: did you
melt with pleasure with your nigger?: repeat in front
of us your gestures, positions, moans, cries till the
moment they caught the two of you fucking!: outbursts of irrepressible sincerity, immediately hidden
behind a rigid mask assumed the moment the higher-
ups made their appearance with reams of paper, a pen,
an inkwell, come on kid, screw up your courage, give
up your false pride, collaborate with us in the common task of rehabilitating you, confess your crimes
freely and openly, trust in the amnesty we've prom-
ised you, listen to the voice of your conscience, all
you need do is help us to help you

imprisoned in a transparent glass cell, ordered to fill
up page after page with heartfelt, vehement confes-
sions, constrained to repent of supposed sins and
abominations, I escaped by thinking of you, my love,
of the fugitive pleasure of our meeting, the lawless

229

passion that united us, the amazing, incredible moments of happiness that carried both of us away, I evoked the memory of your exquisite outlaw's face, your irresistible hair-raising charm, your ferocious, savage air the night we met in the medina of Uxda, you were on the prowl with a militiaman, boots belt insignia leather shoulder strap of the Auxiliary Forces, we gave each other the eye, it was like lightning striking, you magnetized me, the promiscuous pandering of the narrow back street favored our eloquent deaf-and-dumb dialogue, you led me to a dark corner after allowing me to feel the convincing dimensions of your member, cloaked in the pitch-black shadows we panted as we made it while your pal stood waiting on the corner, I was absolutely worn out when I finished, and as you were wiping your cock with my handkerchief, the other guy came and had a go at me, she didn't want to have anything to do with him, your splendor was enough for me, but he insisted and you had a word with me, hwa saḥbi aandu denb tawil, and I was obliged to take him on so you wouldn't be annoyed with me, not realizing that your ex-comrades on duty are lurking about outside your cell, whispering, watching, scheming, noting that you're still lost in dreams, continuing to show no signs of repenting, sitting there for hours on end without writing a single word, all set to run to the

Authorities and rat on you, to invent a thousand wild
accusations, to report exactly how many times I
yawned, my spirits crushed by the wingless unifor-
mity of the daily routine as well, the unvarying ritual
of discussion sessions and work, the false unanimity
of the supposed open meetings of the rank and file,
representing in reality centralization, hierarchy, un-
scrupulous ambition, eagerness to climb swiftly to
the top, to applaud the speeches of the dominations
of the superior choir, to repeat like parrots the watch-
words of the latest, revised edition of the Book, to
feign a nonexistent enthusiasm and joy, to give proof
of an opportunistic servility toward the leaders, to
compose poems, songs, homilies in praise of the Intercessoress, to draw, for the thousandth time, yet
another invariably flattering portrait of her, has she
finally gotten started?, no, she's still beating around
the bush, she's apparently furious, she may well be
planning to double-cross us, to gain time, to establish
contact with the enemy, to dream up new, even more
despicable lies about us, she deserves to go to Avernus
as she did before the next to the last Congress, she
gives the impression that she's trying to test the firm-
ness of our belief in our consubstantial humanism, let
us keep her under the strictest surveillance day and
night, sooner or later she'll reveal herself, remove the
mask that she's clinging to so desperately, her crimi-

nal behavior will leave us dumbfounded, then fluttering away in great excitement to pass the news on from one choir to the next, she's starting, she's taken up her pen, she's tracing or drawing up-and-down strokes on the sheets of paper, wadding them up into a ball, if she tosses them in the wastebasket we'll collect them, we'll be able to have them analyzed, to follow her exact train of thought, as though I didn't already know, as though I were unaware of that inveterate habit of yours of denouncing people, that incurable passion for spying that all of you share, allowed no privacy whatsoever, cut off from the mere possibility of gazing round about you without your eye falling upon their saccharine-sweet faces, their hair almost as pale and washed-out as an albino's, their barren chests, their useless buttocks, their immaculate tunics, enough to drive one suddenly and completely out of one's mind, a boundless horizon, snow-covered vistas, a schizophrenia of fir trees, Arctic desolation

better to write, to smudge the paper, to draw oxygen from my memories, to invent some sort of mocking play on words to bewilder them, that throb in Marruecos marruecos:

ô those maracas
thanks to them I'm Morocco-bound, in both
senses of the word: they're bulging, gleaming,

super-attractive, powerful magnets: an inex-
haustible
storehouse
of divine surprises!
a brainteaser?
yes, and teasing something better still!
if you've tried your hand at this game
you'll know what I mean!
calmly leaving the paper on the table, yawning,
stretching, have you finished yet?, yes, I've finished,
going out for a stroll, getting the kinks out of your
legs, mingling with the militants of a shock brigade
whose chests are dripping with medals, listening to
their stale speeches about this radiant eden and realizing once again that your leaving it is unthinkable
because you aren't living in the present but in the
future, and unless you regain your mortality, there is
unfortunately no one who escapes the future

TO THE DULY CONSTITUTED
AUTHORITIES OF OUR
GLORIOUS CELESTIAL REPUBLIC

on the eve of the bicentennial of the triumph of
our prodigious utopia, in this exciting century

of the edification of a society freed of the vices
and shortcomings of the exploitative systems of
the past, at the end of a decade characterized by
the swift pace of its advances and the attainment of unparalleled goals, at a moment when
our community, enlightened by the constant
reading of the immortal Work of the Supreme
Guide, under the wise leadership of the sublime
Intercessoress and her faithful collaborators of
the executive, is about to undertake new and
victorious endeavors, to disseminate the noble
ideas of an eternally inspiring, invincible doctrine, to consolidate for all time the successes
and achievements of previous plans aimed
at ensuring the perpetuation of the marvelous state of bliss in which we live, within
this bright, splendid, epiphanous perspective
that has enabled us to leap from the past to
the future without being obliged to undergo
the struggles, the tensions, the dramatic con-
flicts marking the present of other historically
doomed societies, the existence of a defect,
however minor and insignificant it might be,
would constitute, in view of the absolute perfection of the whole, a valid reason for concern,
just as the smallest dark splotch within a panorama of such exceptional whiteness would im-

mediately attract the attention of any observer, it would be shocking, it would arouse natural reactions of rejection and fear among the members of our fortunate community, especially if we consider the fact that such a stain might very well spread, contaminate by odious example innocent and pure souls, serve as a fixation abscess of those spiteful dissidents and malcontents whose logical abode would be Avernus had our incomparably magnanimous Supreme Guide not resolved to close it down many years ago

this aforementioned potential threat exists, and since an ounce of prevention is always worth a pound of cure, the object of this brief and humble personal reflection is to warn you of that fact

the stigma, blot, blemish, bad egg, black sheep that is such a jarring note in the marvelous picture of a society embarked upon an amazing process of continual self-transcendence, whereby limits regarded as unattainable are reached every day thanks to the incredible perseverance of choirs inspired by the unsurpassable example of the Supreme Guide and the august head of the Secretariat, this negative element, perversely resisting any sort of therapy,

monstrously persisting in behaving in a selfish,
cynical, and even openly provocative manner,
exists, a fact that I can guarantee with no need
for proof and supporting evidence since that
negative element is myself

despite the incredible efforts of a number of
heroic comrades who take turns at my side
night and day with the aim of fraternally per-
suading me to abjure my abominable errors,
with a steadfastness of purpose, a dedication, a
fearlessness, and an altruism that arouse my admiration and enthusiasm, I have remained deaf,
inaccessible, and indifferent to their irrefutable
arguments, to the exceptional goodness and
generosity they have so prodigally made manifest to me

I am unworthy of belonging to a collectivity
whose lofty moral standards are a clear demonstration of its exemplary, unsurpassable nature

the baseness, wretchedness, perversion that I
have known in a defective and dying world,
inevitably fated to disappear and be replaced by
the superior dynamics that we incarnate are
more attractive to me than the promise of ineffable, sempiternal happiness that you vainly offer me and have offered me

a single moment of sensual pleasure, the memory of full round lips, a fierce, feline gaze, a magnificently hung male apparatus cancel out in one stroke your marvelous promises and realities

I want to be a hundred percent mortal, to fall into the dungheap of History

give me back my old age, my wrinkles, my toothless mouth, my worn-out vagina, my battered anus

this is my self-criticism, and I shall not recant it trusting in the filthy truth of my reasons I place my destiny entirely in your hands

expressions of surprise, astonishment, stupefaction, rage, repugnance successively crossed the faces of the avid readers of the letter: those who had seen it flew to the others with their version of its contents, deliberately exaggerating its scandalous import, adding details they had invented out of the whole cloth, failing to use, as regulations required, the normal hierarchical channels to transmit the news: the idea of a possible conspiracy took hold: rumors that spread like wildfire caused enormous consternation, there were whispered discussions as to the advisability of informing the Supreme Leader, of apprising the remote head of the Secretariat of this unprecedented turn of events: the gist of the letter was too serious, its effect on Her might be disastrous, nobody was willing to take the responsibility, nobody dared bell the cat: in vain they sought inspiration in the clairvoyant pages of the Book, prayed more fervently than ever, repeated the maxims in chorus: no such case had been foreseen, and on discovering this, their feelings of frustration and impotence gave rise to a vague sense of despair that soon bordered on utter demoralization: several members of shock brigades reacted hysterically, and according to what she said later, clawed at the glass cell in which she was confined: the Intercessoress was stricken with one of her usual migraines and immediately, by unanimous consensus, the solution that seemed most sensible was adopted: did she want to give up ad vitam aeternam the great benefits and gifts that had been lavished upon her?: did she prefer wretchedness, old age, decadence in a fallen world inexorably headed toward destruction?: well then: let her go down there: her wishes would be fulfilled!

solemnly, irrevocably, the decision was adopted to expel her

from this point on the explanations vary appreciably: some say they saw her land in the cemetery of Bab

Dukkala, full of energy, in high spirits, youthful, optimistic despite her years and the difficulties of a long, exhausting journey: the story has it that she made her home base there till her death, hanging about the entrances to military barracks, offering her services, devoutly, fruitfully, tirelessly fulfilling her apostolic mission

others say she resides in Sidi Yusuf Ben Alí, dresses like a Moslem woman, and walks along the wall each day, headed for the tannery of Bab Debbagh in the hope of meeting her old flame

still others claim that she lives or lived happily with the latter till death overtook them, but I, the European halaiquí who have told you this story, assuming different voices and roles in turn, making the characters fly from one continent to another without having moved for an instant from the fraternal group that we form, am not able to confirm the truth of any of the versions

nonetheless, there are certain things that my craft requires of me, and since my audience expects a happy ending, I am inclined to support the most heartwarming hypothesis: I believe that, in fact, the two of them are enjoying a most pleasant and well-deserved rest that counterbalances the unsettled life they led: thus leaving my hearers with a fleeting taste of honey, rewarding them for the fidelity and patience with which they have remained in the halca, that tiny little island of freedom and rejoicing in an ocean of wickedness and misery, giving them and giving myself the necessary strength to complete the day's journey, to gather up our belongings and prepare to move on, to seek shelter, to lull ourselves to sleep with the idea that tomorrow everything will be better and they will still be with you, as will I, all ready to invent new and even more marvelous adventures, finding a welcome refuge, if it be God's will, in the free and easy, kindly tolerance of the public square

A READING OF THE SPACE
IN XEMAĀ-EL-FNĀ

in order to make the first contact easier, the Guide
Bleu recommends going up to the flower-covered terrace of a café in the late afternoon, as the sun is
setting the urban landscape afire and it is possible to
watch the city's ubiquitous improvisation of its festival in all its splendor
Fodor, on the other hand, proposes a morning incur-
sion by way of Bab Fteuh, so as to get a firsthand idea
of the incredible bric-a-brac for sale in its markets
more prudent, Nagel, Baedeker, Pol suggest a casual,

discreet approach, sneaking up on it quietly and unobtrusively from the sidelines and letting oneself be
swept along by the crowd until one finds oneself
unexpectedly inside
couleur locale breakaway fascinación
and yet
all the guidebooks lie
like a spider, like an octopus, like a centipede slithering away, wriggling and writhing, escaping one's embrace, forbidding possession
there is no way of getting a firm grasp on it

an agora, a theatrical performance, a point of convergence: an open and plural space, a vast common of
ideas
peasants, shepherds, soldiers, tradesmen, hucksters
who have flocked to it from the bus terminals, the
taxi stands, the street stops of jitneys poking drowsily
along: coalesced into an idle mass, absorbed in contemplating the daily hustle and bustle, taking refuge
in the anonymous freedom and permissiveness of
these surroundings: in continuous, capricious movement: an immediate contact between strangers, a forgetting of social constraints, identification in prayer
and laughter, the temporary suspension of hierarchies, the joyous equality of bodies

strolling slowly along, without the slavery of a time schedule, following the wayward inspiration of the crowd: a traveler in a constantly moving, vagabond world: attuned now to the rhythm of all the others: in graceful and fruitful nomadism: a slender needle in the middle of the haystack: lost in a maremagnum of odors, sensations, images, multiple acoustic vibrations: the dazzling court of a kingdom of madmen and charlatans: a poverty-stricken utopia of absolute equality and freedom: migrating from group to group, as though wandering from one pasture to another: in the neutral space of chaotic, delirious stereophonic sound: tambourines guitars drums rebecs cries of street vendors speeches suras screams: a fraternal community with no notion of asylums, ghettos, outcasts: lunatics, freaks, monsters set up camp wherever they choose, proudly exhibit stumps and scars, rebuke the passersby with furious gestures: blind savonarolas, crawling beggars, reciters of the Koran, men possessed, energumens: each with his particular obsession riding on his back, shielded in his madness as though it were a conch shell, breasting the tide of an indifferent, mocking, compassionate crowd the multitude overflows into the traffic along the thoroughfare, surrounds the cars and the jitneys, hems in the little carts of the delivery boys, blockades the flocks of sheep and goats, takes on the appearance of a huge demonstration without a purpose, of a popular army without ranks or hierarchies: bicycles steered by aerialists, packs of donkeys loaded with baskets, buses whose parking maneuvers give rise to feelings of pity, the clumsy movements of a defenseless beached whale: speed, strength, power forced to obey majority rule: the impotence, the futility of horns and engines: the revenge of the spontaneous, the motley, the proliferating on the ordering of all things according to strict classes: a no-man's land where the body is king and the effigy hung on buildings and lampposts a grotesque, faded puppet

survival of the nomad ideal as a utopia: a universe without a government or a leader, the free circulation of persons and goods, land owned and used in common, the tending of flocks, sheer centrifugal force: the abolition of private property and hierarchy, of rigid spatial boundaries, of domination based on sex and age, of the ugly accumulation of wealth: emulating the fruitful freedom of the gypsy who respects no

244

frontiers: encamping in a vast present of quests and adventure: making no distinction between sea and land, navigating across the latter in the lighthearted mood of the fisherman: creating structures to welcome the world-wanderer, free ports for trading and talking together, marketplaces, little bazaars for the exchange of ideas

seafaring nomads or fishermen sailing across sand: palm groves in the middle of the desert: islands of green in an ocher ocean, with a rough, rippling surface: a groundswell that curls the crests of the dunes: tree trunks with the tops lopped off, towering like topmasts: tiny caravans like flotillas struggling to make headway in heavy seas

analogies between desert and ocean: endless space, isolation, silence, the imbricated patterns formed by waves and dunes, boundless, unbridled freedom, brightness, sharp clarity, absolute purity

an aleatory relationship with the elements: a common dependency on wind and rain, sun, moon, stars, storms

ancestral caution, experience, wisdom in the face of climactic traps and snares, sudden treacherous changes in the sky

a keen sense of direction, a similar reading of the
stars, an acute sensitivity that heads straight for the
school of fish or the trickle of water lying ahead
mobility, courage, uncertainty, solidarity when danger threatens, stamina, moderation, spontaneous and
fraternal hospitality

a portable business establishment: peddling reduced
to its simplest expression: a threadbare carpet or a
little straw mat: odd, meager means of livelihood: a
little metal box containing a handful of roots, a worn
pack of cards, an anatomical plate in color, a treatise
on the art of love and aphrodisiac recipes, an old,
well-thumbed copy of the Koran: Aladdin's lamp at
nightfall, a protective parasol perhaps, open like an
umbelliferous mushroom, beneath which a gnome in
felt slippers and a peaked cap shelters himself as best
he can from the sun's despotism

the proverbial difficulty of listing all the things that
space engenders
knicknacks, miscellaneous utensils, odds and ends
swept along narrow streets and main arteries by a
violent maelstrom: countless objects of every sort and
description wherever the eye happens to land: an

utterly mad proliferation of useless goods: advertisements and images of consumer products to entice the possible buyer

patiently setting down nouns, adjectives one after the other, parts of speech fighting a losing battle with the perfect simultaneity of the photograph: chasing after the same effect in vain, like a traveler who misses the train and stands on the platform panting grotesquely till he runs out of breath

artifacts, gadgets, products filling the vacuum, materially occupying the entire urban landscape, pouring out in a cloying stream from bazaars and stalls, overwhelming the visual field to the point of nausea

pyramids of almonds and walnuts, dried henna leaves, Moorish shish kebabs, steaming caldrons of harira, sacks of broad beans, mountains of sticky, filthy dates, carpets, water jugs, mirrors, teakettles, trinkets and baubles, plastic sandals, woolen caps, gaudy lengths of cloth, embroidered sashes, rings, watches with colored dials, faded postcards, magazines, calendars, cheap paperbacks, fat sausages, pensive sheeps' heads, cans of olives, bunches of mint, sugarloaves, blaring transistor radios, kitchen utensils, earthenware pots, couscous bowls, wicker hampers, leather jackets, straw bags from the Sahara, esparto-grass fruit baskets,

Berber handcrafts, stone figurines, pipe bowls, sand roses, fly-specked pastries, sweets tinted violent colors, lupine, garden seeds, eggs, crates of fruit, spices, jugs of sour milk, loose cigarettes sold separately, salted peanuts, wooden spoons and ladles, miniature radios, cassettes of Xil Xilala and Noss-el-Ghiwán, tourist folders, passport cases, photographs of Pelé, Um Kalsúm, Farid-el-Atrach, His Majesty the King, a map of the city of Paris, a bizarre Eiffel Tower
adding
in homage to Jacques Prévert
to this odd inventory of miscellaneous items
the symbolic presence
of a RATON LAVEUR

the comfortable garments enveloping the Arab body: the freedom of expression offered bodily members by the flowing robes, physiques hinted at by the softness and suppleness of cloth whose folds set off curves and hollows more suggestively and effectively than if they were nakedly displayed: a clever, elusive game of hide-and-seek in the communal anonymity of the public square: faces, legs, waists, bosoms delicately outlined behind chaste veils and kerchiefs, severely unadorned caftans, decorous almalafas and fuquías:

248

thighs in helicoidal rotation round the shadowy center of the target, hips waggling with the rhythmical
movement of connecting rods, breasts under only the
very slightest tension quivering joyfully: currents,
vibrations, rushes of blood immediately reflected in
parallel and opposite tumescences, concealed beneath
the coarse-textured djellabah or the ample, prudent
burnoose: inguinal cones that transform the fabric
into a Bedouin jaima that discreetly shelters the erect
tentpole: in an indiscriminate mingling that lends
itself to unavowable secret pandering, bawdy gusts of
wind, subtle maneuvers of pollination: a little market
based on supply and demand in which the bargain is
sealed with smiles and signs, and experts in the field
of spontaneous semiology, the prospective participants in the deal decipher desires and impulses by way
of the reading of each other's garments against the
light

amid burnooses, fuquías, jeans made in Korea and
Hong Kong, T-shirts bearing the official seal of Yale,
California, Harvard, New York University
it is pointless to ask those wearing them whether they
are graduates of these institutions: most likely only a
few can even read the letters of the Latin alphabet
the ridiculous prestige of a superannuated system

twinkling brightly across a distance of countless
light-years, like the glow of a planet blown to bits
long ago, of a falling star long since dead
the vanity of a culture turned into a gadget, cut off
from the roots from which it ought to be drawing its
vital sap, unaware even of its own dramatic non-
existence

the conception of wearing apparel as symbol, reference, disguise: the variety and the splendor of
the dress permitted in the brief parenthesis of a holi-
day celebration: the temporary shedding of one's ordinary garments and social personality: changing
one's clothes so as to change one's skin: being, for a
few short hours, a nabob, a world traveler, a king:
staging a performance for oneself and others
(elderly men dressed in white from head to foot, girls
with silver earrings and bracelets, delicate, transparent almaizales, a profusion of new sashes and slip-
ers, turbans like gracefully coiled serpents)
a theatrical spectacle: the calls of muezzins in the
minarets of the mosques as an accompaniment in the
background: shoddy footlights, stage sets, backdrops:
joining in the rejoicing of the chorus bidding farewell to the fast of Ramadan

the fierce rivalry of the halca: multiple, simultaneous attractions: the frank abandonment of this or that spectacle by a crowd continually in search of novelty, the infectious excitement of the knot of onlookers gathered together a few steps farther along: the need to raise the voice, argue, polish up the come-on, perfect the gesture, exaggerate the grimace that will capture the attention of the passerby or irresistibly unleash his laughter: capering clowns, agile tumblers, Gnaua drummers and dancers, shrieking monkeys, the pitches of healers and herb-sellers, the sudden bursts of sound from flutes and tambourines as the hat is passed: immobilizing, entertaining, seducing an eternally drifting audience seeking only to be diverted, magnetizing it little by little and attracting it to one's own particular territory, wooing it away from a rival's siren song, and finally extracting from it the shiny dirham that will be the reward for physical strength, perseverance, cleverness, virtuosity

a comic, smiling parody that mirrors in reverse the agitation, the frenzy, the commotion of operations on the New York Stock Exchange during its frequent

gales of euphoric optimism or gusts of panic, when
the Dow-Jones average suddenly shoots upward or
suddenly tumbles amid the frantic shouts of customers, the dizzying shifts in the figures posted on the big
board, the frantic clatter of the stock tickers, the
rapid-fire gibberish of the professional traders
local color à rebours: the awesome bedlam of whites

sitting on the ground, a simpleminded soul strokes
the strings of his rebec, lovinglycradling it like a wet
nurse: the crowd censors out his humble, wretched
presence, hurries on past him, engrossed in its affairs,
allowing him to enjoy a diaphanous transparency,
abandoning him to his monotonous, obsessive strum-
ming: lips set in a perpetual smile, a strabismic gaze, a
life projected toward an impossible horizon: charitable folk keep him alive and he accepts his destiny
with cheerful resignation: coming into this world to
rock his instrument to and fro, to play sour notes, to
repeat the same gestures endlessly, to occupy day after
day a modest gap in the common space of the public
square

a veiled woman plays a game of solitaire as she waits
for a nibble from a client: an old man draws a graffito

in chalk as he recites a sura half to himself: the chorus
of beggars chant, over and over without a pause, fi-
sabili-l-lah and smilingly shake their alms boxes: the
sun beats down on their heads, chisels and accentu-
ates the lack of expressiveness of their features,
sculpts and immobilizes their forced smiles, makes
them blink (or is it the swarm of flies that is responsible?) as though they had recovered their sight despite
their empty eyesockets, their glass eyes, their hid-
eously scarred eyelids

the brotherhood of the Ulad-de-Sidi-Hamad-u-Musa
suddenly huddles together to form the great pyramid: youngsters scramble up the stirrups of hands,
hoist each other up with rapid gestures, find a firm
foothold on the shoulders of the men down below
who are bearing their weight, give a helping hand in
turn to those who are to mount to the very top: a
rigid hierarchy based on weight and age: from the
robust adults at the base to the frail child who ingen-
uously waves to his retinue of admirers from the lofty
height of his wondrous throne: the bright colors of
short jackets and balloon trousers blaze, and in obedience to a signal from the leader, the hefty acrobats
at the bottom slowly shift the axis of the entire pyramid so that it makes one, two, three complete circles

in lithe and graceful equilibrium: as meanwhile the audience cheers and applauds and adds a few dirhams to the brotherhood's slim, modest peculum: as they drop off the pyramid, the youngest ones begin their acrobatic exercises to the throbbing beat of a drum: supple aerialists perform their daring turns in a swift, weightless whirlwind: cartwheels, somersaults, perilous leaps, defying Newton's laws, making a mockery of the ponderous earthbound apple, proving the volatile nature of the bodies of children forged in the rigor and austerity of lives without protection or families, left to rely on their own resources from their tenderest years onward: others bend their trunks back, expand their rib cages like accordion bellows, thrust their heads between their legs, put their limbs out of joint, subject themselves to disastrous contortions, appear to fold up by doubling over backward: camp chairs that unexpectedly metamorphose, assume human form once again, and even have the courage to force a weak smile as they catch sight of the admiring glances of the audience

the circular empty space, the resounding vacuum of the Gnaua rite: an area vacated by the insistent beat of a drum in order to present the severe rigor of their immutable spectacle at the proper distance: a

254

group of actors standing in a row, immaculate trousers and blouses, smooth, dark legs, unadorned and
quintessentially naked: the dervish who is that day's
principal performer bares his gleaming teeth, whirls
drunkenly round and round in his bare feet, imitates
a Cossack dance, flogging space with the cheery tassel
of his fez like a whip: the compelling rhythm of
clacking castanets causes him to twirl about even
faster and paves the way for the sudden appearance of
the oldest member of the group, as skinny as a handful of vine shoots but possessed of a suppleness and
vigor that absolutely belie his years: a body language
in which muscles are the vocabulary: nerves the mor-
phology: joints the syntax: vibrations, meaning, message convey themselves directly to those watching,
affect their sensory organs, run down their skins in
the form of a tingling sensation, giving rise to a form
of knowledge immediately linked to feeling
an auditory and visual pleasure, a bliss of the senses
that fills the spectator's soul and lingers on long after
the troupe's exit from the scene, like that fleeting
mixture of satisfaction and surfeit experienced by one
who has just furtively made love

two old men with the look of Hindustani fakirs present a rich, motley sample of their useless handiwork

255

on the threadbare carpet covering the territory they have patiently acquired by usucapion: an odd assortment of improvised flower vases made out of bottles, Esso oil cans, tins of Nido milk powder, water jugs, candleholders, each and every one of them topped off with plastic roses insensitive to the round of the seasons, the cruel, continuous assault of the furious sun: the complex structure of their pipes imitates the form of a saxophone, the smell of the incense they are burning is mindful both of a place of worship and a den of kif smokers: dozens of doves flutter about in a flurry of white amid the flower vases, become intoxicated from the fumes of the aromatic resin, alight on the heads of the two old men, peck at birdseed from their gnarled hands, bill and coo at each other, exchange simpering politenesses in the sylvan thickets of their beards, explore, without ever venturing beyond them, the magic limits of the little square of carpet

a strong skull shaved perfectly bare, a thick stubby neck, broad shoulders, coppery skin, thick lips, a Mongol mustache trickling down past his chin, gold-capped teeth
Fantomas
Big Boss

Tarzan
Saruj
Antar
Taras Bulba
he surpasses in both eloquence and height all the
halaiquís staging their acts in the square: his imposing presence and stentorian voice attract each day an
eager audience, willing captives of his fake arrogance:
arms akimbo, legs spread apart, he reels off, like a
schoolboy reciting from memory, the geographical
itinerary of his adventures, his endless string of nick-
names: his explosive, suggestive, mordant way with
words skillfully exploits the resources of popular
speech: a lingo free of all restraint, inhibition, repres-
sion: tales of complicated love affairs, cuckoldry, cunning mingled helter-skelter with verses, obscenities,
suras, bursts of laughter, imprecations, insults: yarns
involving backsides, cunts, pricks that abruptly end
in moral preaching: breaking off between two episodes he goes round the circle gathered about him,
warns the women to withdraw, grabs a youngster by
the scruff of the neck and gracefully sends him flying
with a show of ferocious severity: his fabrications of a
Rabelais redivivus at once extol and make a mockery
of the perils of sexual pleasure: a florid abundance of
allusions, paraphrases, euphemisms adorned with au-
riferous grins, onomatopoeic outbursts, swift up-and-

down movements of his fist with the middle finger of his other hand inserted in it: fornication: Tiznit: fellatio: Tefraút: anal intercourse: Uarzazát: not forgetting the rules of classical oratory, the rhetorical question addressed to his hearers: I ask you: how was young Xuhá able to keep his honor intact the night he slept in a den of sodomites?: the answer: by being clever and foresighted enough to pour thick bean soup down the seat of his underpants beforehand!: a general smile that transforms itself into a gesture of prayer, the ritual accompaniment of the well-known invocation

if Allah does not give a man strength, my brothers, He makes it up to him by giving him cunning: so let us admire His wisdom and give Him thanks!

the roll of drums in the late afternoon, when the copper-colored sun, behind the Kutubia, heightens and enhances the wondrous sights of the city with postcard splendors: the cheerful green of the palm trees in the public park, the bright ocher of private houses and official buildings, a serene atmosphere of imperturbable blue, the distant ridges of the Atlas range topped with plumes of purest white: a luminosity that stimulates and intoxicates, blends with the frenzy of the dances and the hawkers' cries, predisposes the stranger to enjoy a bit of freedom: deep within the vast area established for the pleasure and glory of the senses: absorbed in the rewarding idleness of those who roam about at their leisure, footloose and fancy free: with the certainty of being welcomed with open arms by some hospitable tribe or other: of being, in a word, the master of one's body and a possible candidate for the enjoyment and possession of that of one's male or female neighbor: awareness of one's own attractiveness and youth and desire for the other, or vice versa, translated into a coded language of coughs, winks, smiles: offerings on the open market, within the reach of anyone willing or able to give value for value received: far from the irreducible molecular order of the great industrialized European city: the hostility of the clock, the pressure of time, rush hours, infinite loneliness shared bumper to bumper: separation into individual cells with nuclei incapable of fusion, isolation in crowds of people packed together like sardines: a tool a robot a cipher a machine: incorporality, keeping one's distance, invisibility, ataraxy: the diametrical opposite of the easy familiarity that recognizes no boundaries: of the realm of adventures and encounters, the language of hips, the telegraphy of gestures, festive semierections:

visual and auditory invitations to feel out, to explore, to engage in the furtive chase, to paw with a disembodied hand

a concrete, material, direct fraternity of the group of spectators, physical and sensory contacts in the restless promiscuity of the halca: arms brushing against arms, legs against legs, sporadic touches, cautious approximative maneuvers: antennae directed toward sounding out the intentions of the silent target of this campaign with no fear of slaps in the face or cries of outrage: the prelude to more intensive and daring encirclement tactics: a discreet, continuous advance of one's own trunk in the direction of the coveted posterior: an opulence that is hidden yet hinted at, thanks to the clinging, pandering cloth that permits one to catch a fleeting glimpse of the topography: the ultimate goal the careful insertion of one's convexity in the concavity offered with complicitous delight or a silent sense of guilt: an accentuation at this point of the reciprocal motions, meanwhile maintaining the necessary rigor as one anxiously awaits the outcome: with one's hands in one's pockets, lending aid and support to the rigid and eager device that will permit penetration: shared emotions, furtively concealed from the public eye, deliciously disturbing and intense by virtue of their strict secrecy: the awareness of that excitement of the clandestine celebrated by the poets, pleasure mingled with precaution as when one walks amid sand dunes: an amorous skirmish that through the insurmountable barrier of the cloth inflames and tautens the nerves to a point of impossible fervor: until the enigmatic veiled woman slips out of one's grasp, turns round and disappears on the arm of the spouse to whom she has been unfaithful, without a single backward glance at the anonymous body with which she has nonetheless just coupled

an elderly mime, decked out in a blond wig, throws coins into the air, catches them as they fall, performs magic feats, makes things disappear by sleight of hand, fools the eye, poses for the camera of a tourist couple, demands money from them for the snapshots they've taken, asks permission to kiss their cheeks, and after barely grazing those of the husband, effusively repeats the operation with the man's better half, to the acclaim of a delighted audience that is familiar with the mime's whole bag of tricks and rewards his mocking impudence with great howls of laughter

two clowns do a modest comic turn in rudimentary disguises: donkey's ears, dialogue bellowed at the top of their lungs, both pretending that the other is stone deaf, blows aimed at each other's padded behinds, withering comments and gratuitous insults having to do with each other's sexual or excretory habits

musicians recite chants destined to invoke the favors of a salih with miraculous powers: sinewy flute players, with swarthy complexions and bushy mustaches, accompany the movements of a transvestite in a filmy veil, female garments, and an embroidered sash, whose winks, wagglings, cajoleries, giggles entrance and enchant the spectators who stand rooted to the spot: day laborers, women, little kids, soldiers extend their joined palms in the worshipful gesture of azalá, join in the prayers and ejaculatory petitions, thoroughly enjoying the spectacle as a seeker of alms in a white turban and robe screams at the top of his voice, makes a great show of his emotions, lays on hands, sends old women and young girls on their way with his hasty blessing as he squats on his haunches, feigns beatific fits of ecstasy, writhes theatrically on the ground in convulsions of self-centered piety

installed in the center of the halca, the man proudly empties out his sack as though about to make a careful inventory of its treasures: the reptiles, slowly poking their tiny heads out, tied together by the tail in heterogeneous groups, each strains vainly to escape in a different direction in a demonstration of ineffectual centrifugal force: skinks, lizards, geckos adopting, by reason of their uncoordinated effort to flee, the formless mobility of an organism obeying blind tropisms: their master stuffs them into a wooden cage, and with the gesture of a hardworking seamstress shoving a safety pin into her mouth, places between his lips a lizard missing its tail but still treacherously alive: once he has done so, he stands up, tosses his head back, shakes the braided topknot jutting out of the middle of his shaved skull, and with the reptile still tightly clasped between his lips, proceeds round and round the circle of spectators brandishing the knife with which he operates in vivo: suddenly he stops dead in his tracks, removes the creature from his mouth, holds it tightly in his hand as though about to subject it to another daring vivisection, breaks into a frenetic chant that is half a prayer and half an exorcism: formulas against sickness, the evil eye, accidents, declaimed with closed eyes and abundant fine sprays of saliva: his body suddenly motionless: as the sweat trickles down his face and disappears in his faunlike beard of a splendid goatish male: how to make sure a woman will get the curse?: how to keep an unmarried woman from getting pregnant and dishonoring her family?: simple, perfectly simple: natural medicine, the remedy of the Almighty himself: neither condoms nor the pill nor diaphragms nor jumping off moving trains: lizard-tail extract!

the saurians writhe frantically as though foreseeing their hapless fate: the solemn ritual of their captor: swinging his topknot to and fro for a brief moment, tossing the already mutilated specimen into his treasure chest, choosing another victim, stuffing it into his buccal cavity down to its hind legs, taking the ritual number of turns around the circle, returning to the center, stretching out his hands in a prayerful gesture, and lopping off its tail in one energetic bite of his strong teeth, letting a few drops of blood run down the corners of his mouth, spitting out the severed tail, collecting with the movements of a zombie the generous offering of the spectators

seating himself ceremoniously on the ground, revealing one by one the secrets of a battered satchel, tracing a magic circle in chalk around him, reciting a prayer with extended palms, holding up a bunch of medicinal herbs, passing around an anatomical plate illustrating the state of pregnancy

reeling off the list of dangers lying in wait for the female body, announcing his exclusive possession of the infallible panacea, pronouncing the formulas of exorcism guaranteed to make the devil flee, exhibiting a vial filled with a liquid dyed a violent color, shaking its foaming contents until the bottle overflows, slowly pouring the potion into a glass without ever quite filling it to the brim

sprinkling the fine dust of a powerful talisman into it, stirring the mixture thus obtained with an old spoon, adding a copious emission of saliva, raising the philter to the lips of the first troubled woman to fall for his line, laying his hands on her head in benediction as she anxiously swallows it

health, happiness, her husband's love for the modest price of one dirham as the woman goes off with a prayerfully contemplative expression, as though she had just taken communion

to live, literally, by storytelling: a story that, quite simply, is never-ending: a weightless edifice of sound in perpetual de(con)struction: a length of fabric woven by Penelope and unwoven night and day: a sand castle mechanically swept away by the sea

serving up to an audience ever hungry for stories a familiar theme: keeping up the suspense with a sustained effort of imagination: resorting if need be to the tricks and ruses of the mime: shifting the registers of his voice from bass to tenor

the hearers form a semicircle round the peddler of
dreams, absorb his phrases with hypnotic attention,
abandon themselves wholeheartedly to the spectacle
of his richly varied mimetic activity: the onomato-
poeia of hoofbeats, the roaring of wild beasts, the
screeching voices of the deaf, the falsetto of old
men, the deep booming voices of giants, the weeping of women, the whisper of dwarfs: now and
again he breaks off his story at the crucial moment
and a worried expression comes over the rapt faces of
the youngsters hanging on his every word in the
flickering light of his oil lamp: the travels and heroic
exploits of Antar, the devilish pranks of Aicha Deb-
bana, the tales of Harun-er-Rachid are an invitation
to his young audience to participate actively in the
recitation: they have the same effect as a psycho-
drama, forming through a play of identifications and
antagonisms the rudiments of their embryonic so-
ciability: when Xuhá appears at the palace, at once
clothed and naked, on foot and on horseback, laughing and weeping, a hearty, spontaneous burst of
laughter greets his enterprise and the clever trick
he has played on the sultan: an ideal realm in
which cunning is rewarded and brute force is pun-
ished, the utopia of a just god whose designs are
profound and honorable: the necessary antidote for a
miserable, barefoot existence, empty bellies, a reality

that is cruelly unjust: the hardworking deceiver knows this and eloquently slakes his hearers' thirst for adventure: these little elves in their djellabahs are his only means of livelihood: slowly, with the patience of a spider, he will isolate them from the world: encapsulated in a delicate bubble: his cunning, invisible verbal prison

freeing language, freeing all discourse opposed to the dominant, normal scheme of things: putting an end to the implacable silence decreed by law, superstition, precepts: the authoritative voice of fathers, husbands, leaders, aulic councils of the tribe: a flood of words, violently jerked out of the mouth, like someone pulling out by force a serpent stubbornly holding fast to his viscera: supple, guttural, hoarse, pliable: a language that is born, leaps about, stretches, climbs, becomes spindly: an endless strand of spaghetti, a slender thread, a paper streamer, as in the famous Chaplin sequence: the possibility of telling tales, inventing lies, making up stories, pouring out what is stored up in the brain and the belly, the heart, vagina, testicles: talking and talking, in a torrent of words, for hours and hours on end: vomiting dreams, words, stories till everything has been emptied out: a literature within reach of illiterates, women, the

simpleminded, nuts: of all those who have found
themselves traditionally deprived of the right to express their fantasies and speak of their troubles: condemned to hold their tongues, to obey, to remain out
of sight, to communicate by means of signs and whispers: protected by the semiofficial neutrality of the
place: by the immunity of the jester who speaks harsh
truths from behind the deceptive mask of laughter:
orators without a pulpit or a platform or a lectern:
possessed by a sudden fit of frenzy: charlatans, bam-
boozlers, fast talkers, liars and storytellers each and
every one of them

nightfall: when the bazaar closes down and dancers,
drummers, rhapsodists, flutists take off, literally, for
other parts with their music: the gradual dispersal of
the groups of spectators, an anxious and restless
crowd, like a hive threatened with destruction: the
slow emergence of empty spaces, a complicated web
of meetings and chance encounters on the vast dark
esplanade: dejected women waiting patiently, squatting on their haunches, for a last-minute act of char-
ity: others seeking their plunder on the sly, arranging
a rendezvous by signs: little shops and stalls gathering their goods together and kerosene lamps theatrically lighting new meeting places and points of

convergence: lean-to restaurants that can be quickly assembled and disassembled, traveling kitchens, implements and portable stoves ready for the evening meal: the smells of fried food and soup, cumin, mint tea, awakening the appetite of those strolling by and enticing them into sitting down on the side benches of the stall of their choice

a succession of luminous still lifes projected in a magic lantern: the illustrations of some long-ago edition of The Thousand and One Nights, with merchants, alfaquis, craftsmen, shopboys, students of the Koran painted against a background of caldrons of soup, skewers of grilled meat, smoking frying pans, little baskets of fruit, terra-cotta bowls of olives, plates of bright scarlet salad, depicted with a precision and an eye for minute detail difficult to tone down to achieve an effect of vagueness and distance: a picture of the universe by way of the images of Sheherazade or Aladdin: the entire square condensed within a single book, the reading of which supplants reality

a deserted stage set, rows of shut stalls, remnants of the festival, papers blowing in the wind, excrement and fruit peels, dogs nosing about, beggars sleeping with their forearms resting on their knees and the hoods of their burnooses lowered over their faces

269

a palimpsestic reading: a calligraphy that over the years is erased and then retraced day after day: a precarious combination of signs whose message is uncertain: infinite possibilities of play opening up in the space that is now vacant: blackness, emptiness, the nocturnal silence of the page that is still blank